# PORTRAITS OF FAITH

**REV. CLIFFORD STEVENS**

Our Sunday Visitor, Inc.
Huntington, Indiana 46750

*Nihil Obstat:*
Rev. Lawrence Gollner
Censor Librorum

*Imprimatur:*
✝Leo A. Pursley, D.D.
Bishop of Fort Wayne-South Bend
September 14, 1974

The Nihil Obstat and Imprimatur are official declarations that a book or pamphlet is free of doctrinal or moral error. No implication is contained therein that those who have granted the Nihil Obstat or Imprimatur agree with the contents, opinions or statements expressed.

©Copyright by Our Sunday Visitor, Inc. 1975
All rights reserved. No part of this book may be reproduced or transmitted in any form or by any means, electronic or mechanical, including photocopying, recording or by any information storage and retrieval system, without permission in writing from the publisher.

ISBN: 0-87973-764-6
Library of Congress Catalog Card Number: 74-21891

Cover Design by James E. McIlrath

Published, printed and bound in the U.S.A. by
Our Sunday Visitor, Inc.
Noll Plaza
Huntington, Indiana 46750

764

# FOREWORD

These portraits appeared originally in the pages of the *American Benedictine Review, Chicago Studies,* the *Homiletic and Pastoral Review,* the *Liguorian, Our Sunday Visitor* and *The Priest.* They are, for the most part, studies of figures in Catholic history who have been especially noted for their boldness, courage and ingenuity in furthering the work of Christ. Many of them lived in times of turbulence and change, yet managed to keep their balance, their vision and sometimes their wit intact. A number of them are martyrs who gave their lives for the faith, and some of them are pioneers who broke new pathways and laid the foundations for future developments in human civilization.

It is hoped that these miniature biographies

will move someone to study these remarkable people in larger and more definitive biographies. Some of them, however, do not have biographers and the facts of their lives have been collected from many different sources. Catholic history is full of thousands of others, some known and some unknown, all exemplifying the richness and power of the Catholic heritage.

It is a heritage stretching back almost 2,000 years, touching some of the most remarkable periods in human history and playing its own critical role in the drama of mankind. The few people whose brief biographies are recorded here are not untypical, and the student of Catholic history is constantly unearthing new and interesting people whose histories have been forgotten. These are a few that I have uncovered; maybe someone else can uncover a few more.

Father Clifford Stevens

## CONTENTS

1. ☐ Thomas Merton: Contemplative / 7
2. ☐ The Christianity of Flannery O'Connor / 29
3. ☐ Father Flanagan of Boys Town / 36
4. ☐ Cardinal Spellman / 56
5. ☐ The Santero of San Ysidro / 63
6. ☐ Churchman of the Plains / 69
7. ☐ Archbishop Lamy of Santa Fe / 78
8. ☐ The Amazing Father Kino / 84
9. ☐ The Martyrs of Nagasaki / 93
10. ☐ Francisco de Vitoria: Father of International Law / 99
11. ☐ The Carthusian Martyrs of England / 108
12. ☐ The Emergence of St. Thomas Aquinas / 116
13. ☐ Stephen Langton: Architect of the Magna Carta / 139
14. ☐ Portrait of a Contemplative / 148
15. ☐ The Gentle St. Bede / 158
16. ☐ Joseph the Magnificent / 166
17. ☐ Portrait of the God-Bearer / 173

## CHAPTER 1

# Thomas Merton: Contemplative

No spiritual writer of modern times has had an impact upon the contemporary Catholic like Thomas Merton, or as he was known to many, Father Louis Merton, O.C.S.O. From the first line of *Seven Storey Mountain* to his last article in the pages of *The Critic* or *The Suwanee Review,* his was a voice that was respected, listened to and widely read. His impact upon the present generation was not equal to that of the late '40s and early '50s, but his name and his reputation place him high on the list of influential Catholic writers and thinkers.

His history and his person dominate the religious history of modern times with all the chiaroscuro of the author of *The Seven Pillars of Wisdom,* Lawrence of Arabia, and it is possible that fifty or seventy-five years from now his life will fascinate playwrights and novelists fully as much as that of T. E. Lawrence, or that other amazing inhabitant of the desert, Charles de Foucald.

The Merton mind is quite unprecedented in recent Trappist history and indeed in recent monastic history. He emerges as the only genuine contemplative voice since the golden age of the Cistercian Order, and this Order was unprepared historically and socially for such a mind and such a voice. His pen, however, has left a rich legacy of contemplative wisdom, along with many other very valuable writings, and his writings will stand beside the great spiritual literature of all time. His death in Bangkok in 1968 was noted in periodicals as varied as *L'Osservatore Romano* and the *Japanese Times,* a witness to his universal appeal.

Together with John F. Kennedy and John Courtney Murray, he articulated in mid-century America an idealism and a rationality that was eminently contemporary, genuinely Catholic and painstakingly honest. He separated himself, in thought and in writing, from the trivial concerns and petty loyalties of much that passed for Catholic and monastic, and refused to identify with the outmoded spirituality even of his own Order. In consequence, he became the voice and the symbol of the postwar generation of Catholics, guiding and inspiring a whole generation of young Catholics who were fast losing kinship with the passion and style of their inherited Catholicism. He led many through the uncertain years by a vision of life and holiness that was genuine, bold and thoroughly contemporary. The men of the twenty-fifth and fiftieth centuries, when they read the spiritual literature of the twentieth century, will judge the age by Merton.

Thomas Merton was born in Prades, southern France, in 1915, on the eve of America's entrance into the Great War. His father, a New Zealander, was an artist, and he had come to southern France with his American wife to paint and to drink in the inspiration of the land of artists.

The boy was baptized in the church at Prades, but this was the extent of religion in his early years. Neither his father, an Anglican, nor his mother were professedly religious people and religion was to come into his life indirectly when he would return to France at the age of ten.

At the insistence of his wife's parents, who feared for their daughter and her young son, Owen Merton took his wife and small son back to America, as the United States prepared to enter the conflict. Thus Thomas Merton's childhood was spent on Long Island, and, after the death of his mother when he was seven, he and his younger brother, John Paul, were placed in the care of his mother's parents.

His father during these years was in France and Africa painting, and the young Thomas during the years of his father's absence seems to have developed a marked independence of mind. From his father he inherited the strong intellectual vision of the artist and his whole life would be spent in clarifying and developing a vision of life that was personal and passionate and charged through with an integrity that was akin to being religious.

In 1925, his father returned, somewhat triumphant, loaded down with the fruit of three years of painting. When he returned to Europe in the wake of a small artistic success, his older son was with him.

"When I went to France in 1925 . . . I was returning to the fountains of the intellectual and spiritual world to which I belonged." Thus did Thomas Merton, in later years, comment upon his European experience. This was far truer than perhaps he himself realized.

He would spend almost ten years in Europe, first in France and then in England. He would watch his father die a slow and painful death; and gradually, imperceptibly, he would assimilate the splendor of Europe's past and make his own the spiritual and intellectual heritage that had shaped Europe in the great medieval centuries. The wedding of his father's artistic vision and the contemplative roots of his European experience, deepened in the growing Thomas Merton chasms of thought and feeling rare in one so young. Yet his growing familiarity with the thought and currents of his own age gave a totality to his vision that would burst forth in the remarkable *Seven Storey Mountain*.

It was in France especially, during his years of adolescence, that the medieval heritage struck him with full force. He was to discover in the streets and villages of his native country a warmth, a depth and a beauty that stirred his deepest artistic feelings, yet reached out to something more intriguing. Traveling and living with his father and attending school in individualistic French lyceums, his mind was touched by a theological vision that had shaped the great medieval centuries. He did not become and he never became a romanticist, medieval or otherwise, but he did draw from his European surroundings, the substance of the Catholic vision and his mind was fired very early with a small spark from the flame that had ignited an Aquinas, a Bernard, and a Duns Scotus. Later, when he found that flame glowing in the writings of Gilson, Maritain and T. S. Eliot, the response was electrifying.

In 1928, he accompanied his father to England and began an English education that would take him from an English boys' school to Cambridge. In 1929, his father died, leaving him a small inheritance. He would remain in England five more years; then on the suggestion of his friend and godfather, after one year at Cambridge, he returned to the United States and entered Columbia University. He was nineteen years old, and it was 1934. The next five years would be the most decisive years of his life.

Thomas Merton returned to the United States and enrolled at Columbia University, bursting with idealism, indignation and a keen sense of the misery of life. He seems during these years to have been acutely conscious of suffering and was almost overwhelmed with the helplessness of the human situation. These were the years when war clouds were again gathering in Europe, when the country was recovering from the Great Depression, and when the only articulate voices for social reform and social compassion were Communist voices.

His sympathies were with the poor and helpless and he found kinship with the Communist critique of society. He had a growing sense of social responsibility and this led him to the rallies and conversations directed by the Communist Party. His innate good sense, however, and the honesty that was basic to his nature, soon saw through the facade of compassion that attracted him, and his idealism was to wend its way through other channels. In the literature classes of Mark Van Doren and in the acquaintance of a growing circle of literary friends, he found an honesty and an idealism identical to his own.

He was soon involved in literary activities himself and became art editor for the Columbia yearbook, *The Jester.* Through an odd set of circumstances he became acquainted with a Hindu monk named Bramachari who introduced him to the *Imitation of Christ,* and he found his intellectual interests turning more and more in directions that were theological. By sheer accident, a copy of Gilson's *The Spirit of Mediaeval Philosophy* came into his hands and with his introduction to this volume there began in him a spiritual and intellectual transformation that led straight to Catholicism. He became a voracious and insatiable reader and in a little more than a year became acquainted with everything from St. Augustine to the *Spir-*

*itual Exercises* of St. Ignatius of Loyola. The artistic vision inherited from his father blossomed into the contemplative vision of Aquinas and Dante, with a touch of the mysticism and melancholy of the true artist.

From the moment his passionate mind and its deeply rooted convictions discovered Gilson and the solidity and depth of the Catholic intellectual heritage, it was just a matter of time before Thomas Merton became a Catholic. Several of his close friends were Catholic, and poets and artists he had come to admire, like Eliot, Hopkins and Blake, were infused with the Catholic theological vision. This vision gave him identity and nourished in his own mind a growing awareness of his own significance.

He was baptized at Corpus Christi Church in New York, and his faith from the first moment was mature and passionate, crowning his life and intellect with a joy and a conviction that would never leave him. His mind was sharpened, his idealism became more vibrant and his passion for God, unlocking depths in his own soul he had never suspected, turned with all its intensity towards the blinding light of the beatific vision, which is the goal and substance of the Catholic faith.

In his own words: "And God . . . that center who is everywhere, and whose circumference is nowhere, finding me . . . called out to me from his own immense depths."

In an anguish and an agony, unparalleled in contemporary biography, Thomas Merton began that impassioned search to answer the call.

The anguished loneliness and the aimless gropings of his first years as a Catholic are reflected with painful poignancy in the pages of *Seven Storey Mountain*. His whole life had been crowned with the splendor of faith, but his whole inner world had been shattered by the immensity of his newfound identity. He tried to piece together the patches of asceticism, mysticism, devotion, theology and culture that came with his Catholicism, but succeeded only in making a hopeless jumble of a seemingly unrelated mass of ideas and disciplines.

Through the vast jungle he made his way with the help of good Catholic friends who often neither understood his anguish nor had any knowledge of its intensity. He found solace in the intense poetry of Hopkins and Blake and in the luminous wisdom of Maritain and Gilson, and then discovered the prayerful riches of the liturgy in an English translation of the Roman breviary.

He picked his way cautiously through the huge mansion of the Catholic religion, examining its rooms and surveying its dimensions. Encyclopedias opened vistas to his mind when he read of monks and monasteries, and his growing knowledge of Catholicism became dotted with names like Richard of St. Victor, Carthusian and Camaldoli, *Oxoniense* and *Summa Theologica*, Richard Rolle and Teresa of Avila. The richness and variety began to dawn upon him and he began to search among all this for his niche.

He studied the religious orders and became very close to the Franciscans, finally taking a job with them as a professor of English literature at their college of St. Bonaventure. But even here, he was drawn to their huge library, and although he loved and admired the friars and their life, it soon became evident that this was not his niche. His probing and pondering brought him, at the suggestion of a friend, to plan a Holy Week trip to a Trappist monastery. Then, in his own words: "I went to the library one day and took down the *Catholic Encyclopedia* to read about the Trappists. I found that the Trappists were Cistercians, and then, looking up Cistercians, I came across the Carthusians, and a great big picture of the hermitages of the Camaldolese.

"What I saw on those pages pierced me to the heart like a knife."

Thomas Merton had found his niche.

The contemplative vocation of Thomas Merton came upon him unawares. This simple visit to a Trappist monastery during Holy Week opened to him the vast world of the contemplative life. The simplicity, the solitude, the silence, and especially the total consecration of life seemed an echo of his own deepest idealism and intense spiritual need. There was nothing in his surroundings to inspire such a choice: the Trappists are a unique entity in American Catholic life and their presence is not obvious to the casual observer. In his search for God, Thomas Merton was led to the gates of the Abbey of Gethsemani in Kentucky.

From the beginning, it was the essence of the Cistercian heritage that drew him and he would always be singularly free of the narrow spirituality and "de Rancé" flavor of most Trappist thinking. For that reason, after the publication of *Seven Storey Mountain,* he was considered by many of the older Trappists to be not authentically Cistercian and his influence upon his own Order has been very small. He was more genuinely a disciple of St. Stephen Harding, Bernard of Clairvaux and Aelred of Rievaulx than any Cistercian of the past four centuries. He had no attraction for the seventeenth-century spirituality of most Cistercian manuals and he always found the labored spirituality of Cistercian writers like Vitalis Lehodey rather wearying.

"The thought of those monasteries . . .," he wrote, "shattered my heart. In an instant the desire of those solitudes was wide open within me like a wound."

The Trappist observance had preserved the essentials of the Cisterican and contemplative vision and Thomas Merton found himself a natural child of this tradition. The spirit of St. Stephen Harding and of the great Cistercian adventure of the twelfth century rings through these words of *Seven Storey Mountain:*

> "They were poor, they had nothing, and therefore they were free and possessed everything, and everything they touched struck off something of the fire of divinity. And they worked with their hands, silently ploughing and harrow-

ing the earth, and sowing seed in obscurity, and reaping their small harvests to feed themselves and other poor. They built their own houses and made, with their own hands, their own furniture and their own coarse clothing, and everything around them was simple and primitive and poor, because they were the least and the last of men, they had made themselves outcasts, seeking, outside the walls of the world, Christ's poor and rejected of men. . . .

"Yet because they had nothing, they were the richest men in the world, possessing everything . . . and they tasted within them the secret glory, the hidden manna, the infinite nourishment and strength of the presence of God. . . .

"Day after day the round of the canonical hours brought them together and the love that was in them became songs as austere as granite and as sweet as wine. And they stood and they bowed in their long, solemn psalmody."

After his baptism, he had plumbed the depths of his newfound faith and his circle of Catholic friends had grown: Robert Giroux, who later became a partner in the publishing firm of Farrar, Straus and Giroux; the Baroness Von de Hueck, founder of Friendship House; Dorothy Day of the *Catholic Worker;* Dan Walsh, a professor of philosophy at Columbia, and, of course, the Franciscans at St. Bonaventure's.

He also plunged into literary activities and began writing book reviews for the *Herald-Tribune* and the *New York Times*. He completed a novel and became acquainted with a literary agent who sent his manuscript to several publishers.

But during all this time, he was thinking, pondering, searching and probing the vast world of the Catholic faith that had become his heritage. With a singleness of purpose and a bold independence that was deeply ingrained in his character, he chose to become a Trappist. It was the natural consequence of his own idealism, and yet was only the beginning for Thomas Merton.

In the marriage between the Merton mind and the Cistercian tradition is to be found one of the most powerful combination of forces in the history of spirituality. The only other parallel in history is the joining of the Aquinas mind and the Dominican tradition in the thirteenth century.

Thomas Merton found his natural habitat in the Cistercian life even though he would always have strong reservations about much Cistercian thinking. He came into Cistercian life at a most propitious time, just before a burst of vocations would expand the life to every corner of the country. He came at a time also when Cistercian thought and spirituality had long been submerged in the worst elements of a late Renaissance devotionalism. For centuries, the Cistercian Order was an isolated fortress, speaking to itself, guilty, in its spirituality, of stagnant inbreeding and spiritual bullying, living on the spiritual scraps of past centuries, its spirituality wrapped up in the style and prejudices of the late seventeenth century. Thomas Merton did not conform to this pattern. And he came at a time when the Order was in desperate need of an articulation of its ideals that was passionate, bold and thoroughly contemporary.

In Thomas Merton, the Cistercian tradition found an articulate voice, wielding a powerful influence for good, bringing to his Order in his own person, a respect it had not had for centuries, burying forever the myths and dark fables of "Memento Mori" and Maria Monk.

He found in Cistercian life the deep streams of its own authentic traditions and opened them once more for his own Order and for the world. First, however, he nourished himself upon them, he planted his intellectual roots and his vibrant idealism in the soil of the Cistercian heritage and when he began to write, his voice had all the power and conviction of a Bernard of Clairvaux. He did not, however, conform to the traditional "Trappist" pattern; ever the contemporary man, he remained so even in the cloister, an inhabitant, but not a product of his environment.

There is evidence, however, that his early years in Trappist life were years of profound peace and joy. He lived the quiet peaceful life intensely, and his contemplative mind blossomed into a spiritual maturity vibrant and intense. Wrapped in solitude and silence, nourished by the long hours of sung prayer and quiet study, he walked in the footsteps of the first Cistercian fathers, quietly feeding a smoldering fire that would burst upon the world with unexpected force and brilliance.

Conscious of his literary ability, his abbot assigned him to translate certain works from the

French, and even commissioned him to compose a life of a holy Cistercian nun who had died in Japan. Reluctantly, he was given permission to publish some of his poetry. Then, in 1947, a huge manuscript was sent to a literary agent in New York, Naomi Burton, who had been charmed and impressed with his first attempt at a novel. She and Robert Giroux, an editor at Harcourt, Bruce and Company, sat down to edit the most amazing piece of writing that had yet come into their hands. In a few months, *Seven Storey Mountain* burst upon the world like a bombshell.

*Seven Storey Mountain* became an immediate best seller. It voiced the concern and the aspiration of the postwar generation and the anxieties of people caught in the upward surge of the postwar secular city. Its author was compared to Augustine, Bernard and Pascal; his spiritual testimony placed beside the *Confessions* of St. Augustine and the *Apologia* of Newman. His prose was praised, his mysticism welcomed, his voice became a respected oracle of spiritual truth. Some theologians questioned his theology, some spiritual writers criticized his spirituality; none questioned his literary ability, and the Catholic community rejoiced that it had a master of style, the first universally praised wielder of the pen since Newman.

The work itself was a rare collection of insight and conviction built upon the skeleton of his own personal history. In it, he is seeking his true identity through all the struggles, decisions and wanderings of his early years. It is a synthesis of his thought and conviction and there emerges from this personal history, a deep sense of fulfillment, absent from all his future writings.

The book was translated into most of the modern languages, and for one generation his name was a household word in the Catholic community.

On the heels of *Seven Storey Mountain* came a rich harvest of writings: *Waters of Siloe* (1949); *The Seeds of Contemplation* (1949); *The Ascent to Truth* (1951); *The Sign of Jonas* (1953); and *Bread in the Wilderness* (1960). Within a few short years, he produced a remarkable output of superb writings with a knowledge of history and theology that was truly fantastic.

The fruit of his own search for God and of his Cistercian contemplative life, his early writings ring with a conviction and strength of language, with honesty, clarity and brilliance of intellect. From the silence of his cloister, he began to share his treasures of truth with the world.

*Seven Storey Mountain* was written when he was scarcely thirty years old, and as he dug deeper into his contemplative existence, reached the priesthood and lived the fullness of his consecration, his joy and peace spilled over into his writings. He would never, in the same way, reach the brilliance and scope of *Seven Storey Mountain*, but the fruits of his contemplative spirit would continue to nourish Catholics in all walks of life for a whole generation. The attention of people of all faiths, in all walks of life was drawn to the Cistercian cloister, and Trappist novitiates were full, many candidates drawn by the mystic *caritas* of this voice from the silent cloister.

The fame of *Seven Storey Mountain* made *The Seeds of Contemplation* an immediate success also. Its charm and its accurate mirroring of the spiritual combat have not lessened with the years, and it may yet become the most enduring of his early writings. It is incomplete in its vision of man and immature in its judgment of "the world," but its passion and its pain make it the common voice of the seeker of God, and the peace and tranquillity of its mood bring something of the monastic quiet to the reader. In it, Thomas Merton is neither prophet nor poet, but simply the monk, sharing his cloister with the world. For thousands of Catholics, it gave new insights and a new dimension to holiness and opened their minds to the sublimity of their faith.

The Merton mind has been called "Augustinian" and "Scotist," but it is hardly that. This designation has no validity in this age of theological brilliance and Scriptural renewal. The Merton mind was supremely contemplative, less exuberant than John of the Cross, less scholarly than Augustine, and less adventurous than Thomas Aquinas. It had qualities uniquely its own and a rich prose in which to clothe itself.

Emerging, first of all, with an instinct for the prophetic, the mind of Thomas Merton sharpened into a theological tool of great precision, master of a theological house that had not been occupied for centuries, a brilliant light for a whole generation of Catholics who felt the weight of his mystic passion and the glow of his radiant *caritas*.

His mind was prophetic and utopian, supremely at home in the world of ideas, exuberant to the point of lyricism and allegory, a mind which always sought the higher ground.

Like St. Stephen Harding, the founder of his Order, Thomas Merton has been called an intellectual. Traditionally, within the conventional Cistercian framework, there has been no place for the "intellectual." The Order boasted and cultivated what has been called "rustic simplicity." The intellectual was tolerated as the necessary burden of the monastic administrator and thus the Order was deprived of the insights, the enthusiasms, the rooting force of carefully wrought thought and the articulation of the Cistercian ideal that was contemporary, impassioned and relevant.

In Thomas Merton, this tradition of the Order died, and his mind embodied almost alone the whole idealism of the Cistercian tradition. Before his coming, *will* and *will* alone was the unifying force of Cistercian life, the will of abbot or General Chapter. Ideals were simply a matter of personal piety.

In Thomas Merton, the Order recovered *mind* as a unifying force and the Order is beginning to recover, as a whole, a concept of its own traditions and a sense of identity which alone can carry it forward into the age of *aggiornamento*.

His detachment from conventional Cistercian

spirituality was part of a deeper set of detachments, and is the one saving feature of contemporary Cistercian thought. The sham, pretense and ritualistic loyalty to timeworn phrases and narrowly monastic concepts is one of the unsavory features of much Cistercian literature. By his coolness to all that passed for conventional Cistercian thought, he brought a freshness and a freedom and a wholesome maturity into Cistercian life and focused attention upon the essentials of the Cistercian vision.

This single-handed achievement, in the midst of the turmoil and upheaval in Cistercian monastic life, was scarcely appreciated by his own generation of monks and may go unnoticed for several decades. But when the Cistercian Order as a whole recovers a sense of its own identity and articulates for itself the essentials of its monastic traditions, the insight and intelligence of Thomas Merton will take on truly massive proportions.

The Merton intellect was an educated instrument of rationality and insight that met a theological vision full force and never stopped plumbing the depths of that vision. It was ideological without being pedantic, idealistic without being pretentious, and honest without being arrogant. His mind was superbly critical in the tradition of Aristotle, Thomas Aquinas and George Bernard Shaw, but the rational edge of his thought was tempered by an innate courtesy reminiscent of St. Stephen Harding and Cuthbert of Lindisfarne.

His insight was derived from a vision of the

whole, rare in contemporary theological thought, and his intellectual passion resplendently portrayed the human drama which is the heart of all theology. Gifted with an extraordinary capacity for synthesis, his historical, theological and literary sense were blended in a marvelous unity and when he turned his mind to genuine theological investigation, as in the *Ascent to Truth* and his later peace writings, the originality of his insights is sometimes breathtaking.

The *Ascent to Truth* is by far the most masterful theological achievement of his early years. It is his most thorough and mature piece of contemplative writing, the most closely reasoned of his books, and the best introduction in any language to the mystical theology of St. John of the Cross. The work is quite unlike anything else he wrote, and completely vindicated him as a theologian. If he had written nothing else, this book alone would stand as a masterpiece of theological science. As a piece of theological writing, it is original, unlike the labored synthesis of a Garrigou-Langrange or the impersonal compilation of a Tanqueray. It is brilliant in its insights and totally devoid of the arrogance and irony of an earlier generation of spiritual writers. Objective, adventurous and passionate, it manifests a discipline of words and exactness of concept usually found in the writings of drama critics or the writers of introductions.

The output of his early years was rich, varied and full of much contemplative wisdom. His poetry exhibits rare moments of beauty and the delicate artistry of his metaphors charms when it does not obscure. Yet in none of his later poems does he express the finely wrought feeling of "To My Brother" in *Seven Storey Mountain*. Although his poetry will be included in anthologies, he was not a true religious poet and nowhere speaks with the power of a Hopkins, an Eliot or a Brother Antoninus. The bulk of his poetry is rather prophecy, caught in tangled metaphors and strained imagery; certainly not his most notable or most genuine work.

In his keen critical sense, in his sober sense of the inherent drama of faith, in his vigorous confidence in the unseen realities that shape human destiny, in his massive awe in the presence of God in human affairs, he recovered for his contemporaries a theological vision of life, and delineated the power and the passion of genuine holiness. It is this that rings through every page of *Seven Story Mountain* and etches itself in words of steel in *The Seeds of Contemplation,* and it is for this he will be remembered when the history of this century and its achievements is written. The *aggiornamento* that took place in his own mind and thought foreshadowed the *aggiornamento* that ripped through the whole Church when a mind not unlike his own ascended that awesome throne, the see of Peter.

It is difficult to write of a man like Thomas Merton because there is always the risk of finding in him whatever qualities you want. Few people ever met him, fewer still knew him well over a long period of time. His friendships and acquaintances were necessarily few.

He seems to have had a rare gift of friendship and the ability to share with others the deep strains of his own mind and feeling. Compassion was his constant companion and the fact that he did not become a priest among the poor or a priestly Peter Maurin is explained only by a deeper kinship that he had, a kinship that is the finest fruit of the gift of wisdom.

If anything, he was thoroughly the contemporary man, with a well-educated mind and a wide familiarity with the men and movements of his own age. Like his contemporary, John F. Kennedy, he refused to be a partial man and like John Kennedy, he became the voice and symbol of a postwar generation.

From his early years, he demonstrated an independence of judgment and a style of life marked with wholesome originality, and one wonders what would have happened if divine Providence had destined him for a position of leadership. By his writings, he made pragmatic the hopes and aspirations of a whole generation of Catholics and those who had never seen him found kinship with his passion and his spirit. This is the image of the man stamped indelibly on his writings and is recorded in the very style and substance of his work. If, as in the case of St. Stephen Harding, the founder of the Trappists, who was faced with a similar task in a far different age, his contemplative vision should have been joined with pragmatic opportunity, the result could well have been something truly monumental for the Church and for the age. But whatever may be the verdict of history, his place in the spiritual lives of the men of his own generation had no equal. He did for his own age what St. Bernard of Clairvaux did for his and that alone is a spiritual testament of great value.

## CHAPTER 2

# The Christianity of Flannery O'Connor

She died in 1964 and her writings were acclaimed by critics as superb literary masterpieces. During the last thirteen years of her life, she was partially crippled, but she continued to write stories powerful in their moral impact. She was southern and she was Catholic, and fiercely proud of both.

Flannery O'Connor was a Georgia girl from Savannah and the family's Catholicism goes back many generations. In 1847, when there were few Catholics and fewer priests in Georgia, Mass was celebrated in her great-grandfather's house in Milledgeville, Georgia, and her great-grandmother gave the land upon which was built the first Catholic church in town. For Flannery, her faith was not just an adjunct to her life, it was the substance of her thinking and the vision that guided her, even in her writings. No one in modern times has delineated, in the world of fiction, the moral imperatives which are the backbone of human life, and Flannery herself left no doubt about this.

"The Catholic sacramental view of life," she wrote, "is one that maintains and supports at every turn the vision that the storyteller must have if he is going to write fiction of any depth."

She was born in Savannah in 1925 and her father, Ed O'Connor, was a real-estate man from an old Savannah family. She went to school at St. Vincent's parochial school and to Sacred Heart school in Savannah and moved with her family to the old Cline home, the home of her mother's family, in Milledgeville, Georgia, when Flannery was about thirteen. It was here that she began writing and where she developed that literary craftsmanship that won her every major literary award in her profession. On her writing table, piled beside her typewriter, can still be seen, in the bedroom where she worked, the Sunday missal she used, her Bible and a breviary from which she prayed. She died in 1964 of a bone disease which had also killed her father.

One of her most harrowing stories, *A Good Man Is Hard To Find,* appeared in 1955 and her portrayal of evil in the story is as chilling as it is masterly, and no one can read it without sensing something of that original sin which is at the bottom of much human misery and is at the heart of Catholic teaching. She was able to penetrate, with the skill of a theologian, into the root reasoning behind the teaching of her faith, and then construct, after the manner of the Gospels themselves, powerful parables that embodied the basic insights of the Catholic vision.

"The Church," she wrote, "far from restricting the Catholic writer, generally provides him with more advantages than he is able or willing to turn to account; and usually, his sorry productions are a result, not of restrictions that the Church has imposed, but of restrictions that he has failed to impose on himself. Freedom is of no use without taste and without the ordinary competence to follow the particular laws of what we have been given to do."

In her writings, and notably in her first work to come to public attention, *Wise Blood,* published in 1952, she combated a certain existentialist point of view which refused to look at the tragedies of human life and draw meaning from them. Unbelievers used eloquence and literary craftsmanship to make disbelief and despair a way of life, and they used language and literature forcefully. Flannery O'Connor opposed them, consciously and deliberately, on the only level within her grasp. She did not try to play the theologian, but a certain theology is implicit in her writings.

"The fiction writer," she said, "presents mystery through manners, grace through nature, but when he finishes, there always has to be left over the sense of Mystery which cannot be accounted for by any human formula."

In her writings, her sensibilities are more than

literary, and she pointed the way to something beyond literature and beyond storytelling. Those who knew her, even those who did not share her faith, were aware of how much her faith meant to her. In 1949, she was a guest of the family of author Robert Fitzgerald in Connecticut, where she did some of her most creative work, but her day began with daily Mass four miles away. She had a pugnacious pride in her faith and was very impatient with theological subtleties which would drain her beliefs of their meaning. Her response to someone who was trying to explain some new theory of the Eucharist was as blunt as it was final: "If it were only a symbol, I'd say to hell with it." To her it was obviously more than a symbol and during the last years of her life, when her suffering tore her apart, physically and mentally, she drew strength from this central mystery of her faith.

In 1951, she was stricken with the strange disease that had killed her father, and many months were spent in the hospital. She had returned to Georgia to the old family home at Milledgeville and never completely recovered from the illness. But she continued to write and her talent was becoming widely appreciated. The late Thomas Merton found in her fiction a contemplative vision in the tradition of St. Bernard and Dante, and T. S. Eliot, no lover of fiction, admired her writing which captured in a modern mold the basic insights of the Catholic heritage.

In 1957, she was invited to Notre Dame to speak on the craft of writing and those who heard her remember her no-nonsense approach to her profession. She had to use crutches, and she spoke of the peculiar and particular background of the Southern writer, especially one who also happens to be a Catholic. The blend, she felt, gave a writer an odd perception of the beautiful and the grotesque, of the seemly and the unseemly. Her own tastes reflected this as well as the style of her writing. In her home at Milledgeville, she kept a flock of ordinary geese, as well as a huge flock of peacocks. The strange contrasts of nature were for her concrete symbols of the stranger contrasts of grace and human nature.

Those who loved her were concerned about her illness, and in the fall of 1957, a cousin in Savannah sent her on a trip to Lourdes with her mother. Her down-to-earth faith did not expect miracles and her natural reticence made her dread any public display of devotion. To please her mother she did bathe in the baths, but saved her energy and her interest for a trip to Rome and an audience with Pope Pius XII, who gave her a special blessing. Her illness did not get better, but it did not get worse, and she found she could spend much longer time writing. She refused to let her illness shake her faith, or destroy her peace of mind and as her friend, Robert Fitzgerald commented: "She felt that an artist who is a Catholic should face all truth down to the worst of it." Without that faith, she might have been just an interesting and curious writer who plied her craft with great exactness; with it, she became a woman whom suffering brought closer and closer to the mystery of Christ, giving her a keener perception of the Supreme Being's hand upon human life.

In 1961, she was awarded an honorary degree from Smith College and in 1964 she won the O. Henry Award for her short-story writing. Her disease seemed to have been arrested after her trip to Lourdes, but in 1963, in the aftermath of a stomach operation, the bone disease with which she had been afflicted returned. She died the next year, mourned by those who knew her, considered by many the literary giant of her generation.

Her best writings try to detect the thread of grace woven into the tragedies and miseries that afflict men, and she tried to delineate the redemptive core at the heart of human action, the face of Christ in the soul of every man. She could write of evil with masterly strokes of the pen, but always against the background of eternity. Hers was not a common piety and her faith made her tough and resilient, and uncommonly honest.

Her greatest book was published after she died. Entitled *Everything That Rises Must Converge,* a phrase taken from the writings of Father Teilhard de Chardin, the book is a collection of short stories in which she celebrates, as one critic wrote, "the violent dialogue of the demonic and the divine." In a variety of ways, and with glowing strokes of the pen, she preaches the basic insights of the Gospels themselves, clothed with the passion and the emotion of her own world. No one can read them without being deeply impressed with her vision of hell and salvation, and the mystery of iniquity which ultimately must lead to our Creator.

She was an uncommon woman, as those who knew her and loved her will attest, and what made her uncommon was her faith, as everyone knew. She lived simply, and she developed her writing craft, looking upon writing almost as a monastic profession, her own divinely given task. She prayed while writing and at every odd moment available to her, and she treasured the breviary which contained so much of the heritage she held in high esteem.

One phrase from her writings sums up the quality of her literary accomplishments and the special task she seems to have pursued in her work. In one of her stories, she wrote: "The trees were full of silver-white sunlight, and even the meanest of them sparkled." She could write of terrible people and harrowing things, almost as Dante could lead his readers into the depths of hell. But, like Dante, she saw behind every human event a kindly Providence and thus in her own way shared her faith with her contemporaries. Her writings are being studied today, not only for their literary excellence and unique style, but also for the vision that she captured in her stories and the convictions she embodied in her work. Those who read her are bound to encounter the faith that was hers, and it is possible that her persuasive eloquence will continue to influence long after her name and her memory are forgotten.

## CHAPTER 3

# Father Flanagan of Boys Town

The shadow of Father Flanagan looms over Boys Town. It is present not only in the chapel where his body rests, or in the sculptured reminders of his person, but in the spirit that hovers over the place. It is imperceptible, perhaps, to those who labor there, so close are they to the memory of the man. But it is there like a pillar of cloud.

Some visitors are unaware that he has been dead almost a quarter of a century, so real is his presence. And those for whom Boys Town is filled with memories expect to see him rounding a corner or walking from his office to the chapel each time they visit Boys Town.

His was a varied personality. No one person could grasp that many-faceted personality, shaped by many battles, educated in a variety of roles before he found his niche. He was at once clever and simple, direct and calculating, gentle and hard, a man of vast experience, yet childlike. He was a product of his age, yet surpassed his age in vision and achievement. His vision, his dreams, his battles and his dauntlessness built Boys Town. Now his body rests, almost like a sentinel, to guard the work and guide its destiny.

It is not so much the historical and geographical milieu in which Father Edward J. Flanagan moved that reveals the man: it is the vision and the conviction that guided him. That vision and conviction was a simple one: the worth of a single human being. This was the sacred law he lived by, and it was a principle that seared itself into his very flesh. This is evident especially in the first days of his work when he moved among those whom others regarded as useless drifters and alcoholics; when he lashed out in anger at those who criticized his labors. When he looked at jobless drifters and social outcasts, he saw men. And he treated them as men, whatever others might think. He had no illusions about success or reform, for this was not his aim. He became their friend, and friendship sets no limits to its service.

In these early days (and in later years, too, by a few) he was considered an impractical fool and even an ambitious innovator. But in spite of his own faults, fears and limitations, and in spite of the sometimes bitter criticisms of his contemporaries, he never lost his esteem for the individual man. He lived ruthlessly the conviction that whatever he did to other men, he did to Christ.

In the living of this conviction, he was indeed rare and unique. Men of every walk of life, of varied backgrounds and faiths, saw something in him that won their devotion and their esteem. Many thought him to be a saint. Thousands of others called him friend though they had never seen or spoken to him. Even his critics admitted a quality they could not define.

Something shone through the humanity of the man, that humanity which charmed some and irritated others; some reflection of God and Christ which burned at the very center of the man's being. It is that which has remained at Boys Town, still casting its shadow after these many years. To understand Boys Town, one must understand Father Flanagan.

The Flanagans were tenants on a farm owned by an English landlord on the edge of the little village of Ballymoe, in County Roscommon, the sheep country of Ireland. The farm even had a name, Leabeg, so much was it a part of the Flanagan existence. The father, John Flanagan, ran the farm with the help of his many sons and daughters, among whom were Patrick, who early in the life of the future Father Flanagan went off to the seminary; Nellie, who was a second mother to the younger members of the family; and Eddie, the youngest boy. The mother, Nora, was the dominant influence in young Eddie's life and he seemed to have developed the habit of consulting her before making any major decision.

The influence of his family upon Eddie Flanagan was profound, deeply woven into the very fabric of his thinking. It was a large family, each member a marked and distinct personality, each one shaped by the tenderness and tensions of family living. Through all his years, Father Flanagan was strongly bound to his family, and Boys Town, in one sense, from the very beginning was a family project.

What is important is that the warmth and tenderness of the Flanagan temperament which became the style of the man, the childlike wonder that endeared him to many, and the resilient toughness and bear-like brusqueness known so well to state officials was the product of Flanagan family living. His brother, Pat, also a priest, inherited more of the brusqueness and had a singularity of mind not so noticeable in the younger brother.

During the critical and competitive years of adolescence, however, Eddie Flanagan was far from hearth and family, and was subjected to the grind and impersonal discipline of a nineteenth-century boys' school, Summer Hill College at Sligo, on the northwest coast of Ireland, far from Ballymoe. From this experience, he learned to dislike intensely institutions of any kind and it is possible to see in his passionate hatred of reform schools some memory of the regimented and severely controlled environment of his Sligo days.

During his early years, before going to Sligo, his brother Pat left for the seminary in Dublin, and Nellie went to New York. Other members of the family married and left home. An old grandfather, deeply loved by the whole family, died. Just as Eddie's four years of schooling at Summer Hill College were over, Nellie returned from New York with glowing accounts of life in the New World. After a long family council, in which Nora Flanagan had the last word, it was decided that Eddie would continue his studies for the priesthood in America. The decision to become a priest had been made early and it was understood when he started his preparatory studies in Sligo that he would follow Pat into the seminary. The decision, however, was the young Flanagan's own. He sailed to America with Nellie on her return trip. Within a few short months, his studies were resumed at St. Mary's College in Emmitsburg, Maryland. Eddie Flanagan was just eighteen.

From the age of fourteen, Edward Joseph Flanagan was a student, and a singularly exceptional one. But he scarcely had taken his first steps of formal training for the priesthood when he had to face the prospect of crushing defeat, something neither his mind nor his idealism was quite prepared for.

He found himself superbly equipped for his chosen vocation and fired with strong and solid ideals, but again and again, three times in three years, his health broke and he had to accept almost complete failure. That the suffering and anguish of these years tempered in him that gentle toughness inherited from his family, there can be no doubt. It also concentrated his attention and his energies almost exclusively upon that inner world of thought and feeling which is the heart of the priesthood and gave him a lonely eminence and spiritual solitude that stayed with him until the day he died. This experience made him independent and decisive. It gave a cutting edge to his mind and manner and set him apart even in the Flanagan clan. This intense concentration of mind and energy upon his own inner world gave him just a touch of the contemplative. He acquired a strength and a stability of spirit that helped him to face even more severe defeats later in life.

His final defeat during these years of preparation was a complete physical breakdown in Rome when the freezing cold and penetrating dampness of the Eternal City struck at his body and withered his spirit at a time and in a place that made the whole experience cruel, meaningless and spiritually incongruous. With a tenacity born of sheer desperation, he clung to his hope for the priesthood. In his battle for health and for his chosen niche in life, he refused to be beaten down or turned back. He learned discipline and a ponderous patience. Out of the darkness and near defeat of these black years, he came at last in 1909 to what he later would consider something close to paradise: the bright and luminous atmosphere of the University of Innsbruck in the Tyrol of Austria, a place carefully chosen for its healthful climate and its scholarly traditions.

Here all the idealism that had been pent up in his battered spirit burst into flame and he worked with a calm and quiet energy that sharpened his mind and his spirit as the climate restored his health.

It is difficult to assess the effect of Innsbruck upon the young Edward Flanagan. His remarkable mind, unhampered by ill health and completely free of the regimentation prevalent in other seminaries of the time, recovered and strengthened a vision of the priesthood unconventional and bold. His contemplative bent found joy in his theological studies and drew from them a sense of identity that shattered any hesitations or fears that still clung to him from his years of defeat.

Hours alone on mountaintops (he became an expert mountain climber and even joined an Alpine mountain-climbing *verein*) nourished in him a deep sense of prayer, and the freedom and personal solitude of these years made him gayer and more contemplative than before. He would always have a peculiar attraction for high mountains and monastic solitudes and at one time even became convinced that his vocation was to be a Trappist monk. His contemplative gifts became tools for a rich priesthood and it was in the vastness and nourishing peace of the Tyrol that the seeds were planted for the daring projects and bold experiments that led to Boys Town. The qualities of leadership which he consistently showed in later years (and the irritating "impracticality" which made him the despair of some of his contemporaries) were the fruit of a theological vision, ruthless and raw, acquired in the Innsbruck years.

In Edward Flanagan, the scholarship and brilliant intellect always were hidden under the humanity and compassion of the apostle. He was never known for his academic knowledge of theologians and schools of theology; all his learning turned to love. However, when the occasion demanded, he could bring forth from the arsenal of his mind knowledge, facts and forceful reasonings shot through with that pragmatic sense which guided all his work. Moreover, he clothed his theology in the human literary tradition of Dickens and Canon Sheehan, and so his scholastic prowess was often hidden even from his closest friends.

The tranquillity of these years never really left him; the vision of his priestly work acquired at Innsbruck was the driving force of his whole genius. He always had a fondness for well-written books, especially of biography and history, which captured an idealism similar to his own, and he treasured the life or words of any man whose aim was a genuine nobility of life. It was this solidly Christian naïveté, profoundly theological and prophetically pragmatic, that was sometimes not quite understood by men of a more practical cast of mind. His insight and his intuition escaped them.

In 1912, he returned to Omaha where his brother Pat had a parish and where his family now lived. Within two years, he would be swept up in a life's work that would draw upon all the energy and idealism he had so scarcely stored away.

The first practical application of the idealism that drew him into the priesthood came in the summer of 1913 when Omaha was flooded with unemployed harvest workers, jobless because of a drought that struck the Midwest. They poured into Omaha by the hundreds and the young priest met them on streetcorners and in back alleys. He began to organize a little campaign to help them and was able to get the cooperation of a few restaurants and grocery stores.

He ran into opposition and found that not everyone shared either his concern or his compassion. To him the issue was clear: What you do to others, Christ had said, you do to Me. "Don't go to extremes," some of his fellow-priests told him. "You don't actually believe those homeless men are Christ?"

He did, and this was the crux of the agony this experience brought upon him. He could not fathom the thinking of those who did not take these words seriously and he proceeded to turn the whole city upside down to help the men. He begged, he borrowed, he went into debt. And then finally he built a temporary home for the men in an old deserted hotel. He called it "The Workingmen's Hotel," but as he himself later wrote: "It was neither a hotel nor for workingmen; in reality it was a refuge for the down-and-out men loafing in the city during the daytime and sleeping in the parks at night." The harvest workers moved on when spring came, and a different kind of occupant took their place. At times, he sheltered and fed as many as 500 men in a night.

It was discouraging, unrewarding work from every point of view. Except for the support of a few admiring friends and the members of his family, he was alone in the work. And his experience with the men made him realize that he was helping them too late. With the thoroughness he had acquired during his studies at Innsbruck, he made an exhaustive study of 2,000 of the men and came to one startling conclusion: nine out of ten of them were products of broken homes; their boyhood had been crippled by a lack of genuine love and the concern of responsible parents.

"I saw," he said, "that this waste of lives was preventable."

His Workingman's Hotel also sheltered from time to time a few newsboys. The similarity of the boys' home situation to the stories of the men was too terrifying for him to overlook. A search for other boys led him to the juvenile courts. Suddenly, unexpectedly, he had five boys on his hands. He found himself torn between the two tasks, either of which would take all the time, money and energy he could put into it. Without hesitation, he closed the Workingmen's Hotel, and in another house in another part of town, Father Flanagan's Boys Home was born. Within a month, he had twenty boys — and it seemed they would never stop coming.

His second work was as unpopular as the first. The first years were crushingly unsuccessful and he barely managed to keep his little home open. Few citizens of Omaha saw any value in his efforts and he was always desperately short of money and often of food. His boys were not welcome in the local schools and his odd mixture of races, religions and national backgrounds was a source of scandal to many of the "better" families of the city. He was carefully and studiously ignored or avoided, a conspiracy of silence which left him quite helpless. At the blackest moment, according to a pattern he would follow for the rest of his life, he launched out into the unknown. He rented a larger home and moved his boys into their own "hotel," with a school of their own. With the help of a hard-working secretary, he began a campaign of publicity and correspondence that made him and his work known throughout the Midwest.

He became as shrewd, clever and calculating as a fox. He watched the local papers for news of celebrities passing through Omaha. From that day forward his home became a mecca for the great ones of the country passing through the city. His name became associated with Jack Dempsey and Babe Ruth, with Will Rogers and Tom Mix. His boys became celebrities in their own right and Father Flanagan lashed back at his critics with the carefully worded slogan that made him famous: "There's no such thing as a bad boy." No one in Omaha believed it at first, but when he had said it often enough and Jack Dempsey and Babe Ruth and Will Rogers seemed to believe it, when his home became a stopping-off place for the great ones of the nation, the city took notice. He became respectable, but support for his work was still painfully small.

And boys came from everywhere: from Montana and Florida, from New York and Oregon — even from Mexico and Canada. Mothers left their baby sons and sometimes their baby daughters on his doorstep. Juvenile judges all over the country sent boys who had been in trouble. Soon the two-story building that had once been a German-American Club was much too small. He tried to bargain and barter for a larger place, but no neighborhood would have him. Then one afternoon he took a ride in the country and came back and told his small staff: "I just bought a farm out in the country. We're moving."

He did not want to leave the city, for he wanted to give his boys the opportunities that life in the city affords, but necessity drove him to a place where he could be completely independent. The isolation plus the largeness of the vision of his work led him gradually to the concept of "Boys Town," but this would only be many years later, when he had transformed the farm on the hill outside Omaha into a self-sustaining and unique little community. For years it was Overlook Farm, and then it was Father Flanagan's Boys Home. Boys Town was just around the corner.

At Overlook Farm in 1921, survival was the key concept. Two hundred boys were scattered through odd farm buildings over the hillside and Father Flanagan himself was housed, office and home, in an old garage. Despair crept into his bones as the number of boys increased and debts mounted. His family feared again for his health. The news seeped into Omaha that the priest would have to close his home. There was silence in the city and then a growing sense of shame. This man who had become a symbol of the city itself was failing because the city had failed him. The city rose up and in a mighty campaign, led by its chief citizens, raised over $200,000. New buildings began to rise at Overlook Farm.

The Flanagan courage mounted the crest of the wave and he sent his boys on a fantastic circus escapade all over Nebraska. With typical Flanagan irony he penned another phrase that only half a dozen years ago would have been meaningless to most of the people of the country: "The Romance of the Homeless Boy." He had transformed a concept into a legend and from that day until the day he died he was occupied wholly in living the legend and making it live for thousands of boys.

Once he had changed the concept, he found himself fighting for individual boys. This brought him into ugly confrontations with state officials and juvenile authorities who did not share his convictions about the patently "bad" boy: the boy who had killed or committed some other crime of violence. To them the Flanagan conviction was criminal neglect itself and they resented the invasion of this "softhearted" priest who could bite hard words into their faces and whose learning and logic could be phrased in language that slashed at their dignity. He stripped the juvenile problem to its naked reality and his fierce reasoning made him a terrible adversary.

There were his years of concentration on the anatomy of juvenile crime. His insights and intuition showed him to be a master sociologist, psychologist and educator. Psychologists who had learned their business by clinical observation and scientific analysis of thousands of cases were amazed at the accuracy of his judgments and the superb skills he had developed. Yet this would always be hidden under the casual Flanagan manner; he never reduced his knowledge to a system.

Father Flanagan's total vision of his work found its full expression in Boys Town, in the concept of the boy, not as a ward of an institution or the inmate of a home, but as a citizen, still in a state of formation, but already possessing dignity and rights. The concept was at work very early when his collaborators were pitifully few and older boys were made responsible for younger boys, and the senior students were consulted in matters that affected the welfare of all.

He reversed the educational concept, prevalent in his own time, of a maximum of discipline and a minimum of freedom. He gave every boy an atmosphere of genuine freedom and a backbone of discipline that led to a growing sense of responsibility. The revolutionary technique worked and Boys Town became a symbol of a new concept in education.

He labored in particular to keep his unique community from becoming institutionalized, for he dreaded the shadow of anonymity that clings to every institution and the facelessness of those who are confined within institutional walls. He labored to preserve for Boys Town and for every individual boy a sense of identity, and in doing so his "City of Little Men" became a unique addition to the legend of America.

Father Flanagan himself became a legend and the legend often was larger than the man. In 1938, the legend became the common property of mankind when Spencer Tracy and Mickey Rooney immortalized Father Flanagan and Boys Town in the Metro-Goldwyn-Mayer motion picture, *Boys Town*. The legend, too, reached out to new horizons in 1946 when Father Flanagan was asked by General MacArthur to travel to the Far East and assist him in rebuilding the youth of war-torn Japan and Korea. Two years later, at the request of President Truman, Father Flanagan went on a similar trip to Europe, where he died in an Army hospital in Berlin.

To many he is still a legend, immovable and immortal, like the stone statue of the man that stands in the middle of Boys Town. To those who knew him he was a rare and unique human being who in his life and work captured something of the greatness of man and reflected something of the greatness of God.

Father Flanagan was neither theologian nor philosopher and he did not articulate a carefully defined ideology. He was in fact singularly impatient with mere ideology and his gifts were rather prophetic and pragmatic. There was a tenacity to his convictions and an almost bull-like clinging to insights and intuitions that others regarded as mere platitudes. Beneath this dogged determination was a deeply ingrained optimism, and what others sometimes regarded as sentimentalism was in reality a rare and vibrant *caritas* nourished and fed by a theological vision that fired his whole priesthood.

From his school days at Drimatample in Ireland, he acquired a fondness for Dickens and always marveled at Dickens' grasp of the human situation. *Oliver Twist* remained for him the classic study of boy psychology and he found in *David Copperfield* insights that were an echo of facts in his own biography.

He differed from others in the social-work field in that he had no particular interest in "social reform" and was not passionately interested in improving social situations. He was interested in individuals, men and boys, and he had little patience with the generalizations and categorizing of the social work sciences. It was his experience that those heavily burdened with the scientific data of the social sciences often lost their common sense and looked upon a degree in their chosen field as a substitute for genuine knowledge born of experience.

He abhorred also the invasions of privacy which became the standard technique of certain schools of social work and his pragmatic optimism clashed with the case-work mentality of many of his contemporaries. He saw farther and deeper than their approximations. For these very reasons, he was highly regarded by individual psychologists, and one of his closest collaborators was the disciple and successor of Alfred Adler, whose child-guidance clinics in Vienna early in the century did remarkable work in the field of child psychology.

He consistently refused to be ideological. His habitat was not the realm of ideas. His whole philosophy was expressed in deeds and action, not in word, and except for the slogan he made famous and one or two classic talks on his work with boys, he left few utterances embodying his thought. He was existential in the best sense of the word, and it was in the white-hot arena of human affairs that his thought took root. His mind is best studied in his work, and Boys Town remains the monument to his thought and to his genius.

While the Flanagan mind was not ideological, he did have an appreciation for genuine scholarship and careful research. He enjoyed conversation with experts in any field and in reading good studies of biography, history and research. His library was a carefully chosen selection of works of good minds at their best and one of the joys of his work was the association he had with men of stature in science, medicine, law, education and government. He himself could write with a pointed and fact-filled pen, as his report to General MacArthur on the youth situation in post-war Japan reveals, but he preferred dialogue to debate, and was at his best with the spoken word and face-to-face confrontation.

The rationale of his work was his own intellectual vision of human dignity and he saw embodied in the boy the whole human heritage inherited from Aristotle through Thomas Aquinas. The sweep of the Thomistic mind and its profound appreciation for solidly human and merely secular values was inborn in the Flanagan mind. Without this strong intellectual framework, unreasoned yet deeply rooted in his thought, he might have been simply one more humanitarian fired by mere social compassion.

The vigor of his mind was evident in his public utterances when he carried on conversations with authorities like Ruth Benedict or former Attorney-General Tom Clark and there are phrases of his report to General MacArthur that show him to be a careful and perceptive observer of the human scene.

His was a religious mind, but it was not loaded with pieties, and was singularly ecumenical long before the word or the concept was fashionable. The Flanagan mind was tough and resilient, shot through with an unusual blend of theological and psychological insight. Upon this insight, he built, not a philosophy, but Boys Town and his insight is embodied in a whole generation of boys.

From the elements of his history, we can construct a portrait of Father Flanagan the man. His was a mind with an instinct for innovation, a mind tempered to bold action and crushing defeat. He was able to weigh well the complexities of the human situation and draw from them the simplicities which are the backbone of human motivation. He comprehended well the tension between public apathy and private feeling and he voiced in his own labors the disquietude of his whole generation; a disquietude, it must be remembered, which sparked the same generation in another part of the world and through the passionate vision of a man named Lenin created a far different social revolution.

His application of Christian principle to the concrete circumstances in which he moved, and the moral fiber and intellectual insight he displayed were classical in the best sense of the term, and the superb artistry with which he maneuvered his work for boys into the public eye and changed by a few bold strokes of imagination the passion and prejudices of a whole generation suggest something more than mere priestly piety and Irish wit. Those who knew him knew the flint-like persuasiveness of his every uttered word, the hardness of his character, and the depth of his feeling; his gift for friendship and his dog-like devotion to family and friends; the tongue that tripped on clichés and fed on platitudes; the gallant, uncalculating and sometimes mathematical mind; the swift, spontaneous and vigorous handshake; the insatiable appetite for work; the unperturbable confidence in the strange destiny that Providence had thrust upon him.

During his lifetime, by his style and by the magnitude of his own achievement, he created his own legend, a legend that is somehow larger than the man, and yet in some ways less than the spirit and vision that guided him.

The grain of his personality was a rare balance of humanity, insight and sheer nerve, coupled with an educated innocence that had looked deep into the inescapable tragedies of the human situation.

He died at mid-century having straddled three continents with his labors. He left behind an imperishable memory and an example of faith and daring that antedated the *aggiornamento* of Pope John XXIII and the monumental achievements of the Second Vatican Council.

## CHAPTER 4

# Cardinal Spellman

Those of us who knew him but little, remember him as the kindly prelate who made the news every Christmas with his visits to Korea and Vietnam. His name was associated with controversial causes and ecclesiastical politics of the highest order; he had become in these latter years the grand old man of the American hierarchy: beloved, criticized, gracious, amiable, identified with the Catholicism of pre-Vatican II days.

Yet we never knew him well. He was an old man by the time our priesthood began and our memories of him are not the best ones. If we would truly understand him, we must see him in his youth, as others remember him. By the time we knew him, he had weathered storms that most of us would be unable to endure and faced challenges that would test the mettle of heroes. He had a gift for friendship that was quite remarkable and those friends he made, who survive him, feel his loss deeply, as he felt the loss of his own friends. The fact that he made friends who ultimately filled high places in the Church and in government was an accident of history. The fact that most of his friends were gone when he passed from the scene obscured the true picture of his face and figure.

If he had died in the blush of his youth, in the wake of his historic dash from Rome with an encyclical from the pope besieged on all sides by a rising and vicious Fascism, the name of Francis J. Spellman would have been immortalized with the Beckets and Mores who died for Christ and His Church. He would have been caught in history, as they were caught in history, in a moment of supreme courage, a martyr and a man for all seasons, the symbol and the glory of American Catholicism.

But it was his destiny to become involved with men, some greater and some lesser than himself, and the articulate boldness of his younger years, expressed more in deeds than in words, has been forgotten. It is naïve to think that he cultivated a shrewd diplomacy and maneuvered himself into the good graces of those in power. This was so contrary to his true self that he never took the trouble to answer the accusation. The fact was that his true worth was recognized very early and he rose from obscurity very quickly because the merit of the man was obvious. He was not of our generation and cannot be judged by it. His greatest work was done when we were schoolchildren and the gold of his personality was seen very early by those who studied with him, lived with him, and grew together with him towards a priesthood that he loved with a passion, and to which he gave his best gifts.

What impressed me in studying his life, was his boldness, his frankness and his complete lack of sham and pretense. As a young priest, this brought him into serious conflict with his own superiors and might have been responsible for his disappearance from a role of leadership in the American Church. His strength was in his loyalty to a vision of man and of the Church, a vision that carried him through the tumultuous '20s and the agonizing '30s and into the barbaric, savage fury of World War II. His name spelled greatness in an era of Churchills and Schweitzers, and his critical work for peace and humanity has been forgotten only because he wished it so. No one knows the number of times he crossed the Atlantic for meetings with the molders of world policy, but no one should underestimate the steely bite of his convictions and the passionate energy with which he faced such monumental tasks.

It would be wrong to eulogize him for the wrong things and it is true that he did not become identified with the causes that fired our own generation. He seems to have never understood the *aggiornamento* and on more than one occasion, he expressed dismay at the directions taken by the Second Vatican Council. He alienated many by loyalties that seemed hopelessly outdated and by a fierce clinging to ideals of a shadowy past. But this was in fact simply his unspoken conviction that he would not fight our battles for us, and that our generation would have to take upon itself the responsibility and the labor of genuine leadership. He had given the example in his own style, and we could read that example however we wished. If our vision was so short that we could not identify with the substance of his thought and feeling, then we were unworthy heirs of a priesthood which he served with his entire being.

Cardinal Spellman did not create and was not the architect of a new age of Catholicism. That glory and that role must be left to others. But he bridged the gap of the years with a patience and a tolerance which gave stability in the midst of change and the quiet familiarity of his face and figure gave a continuity to the *aggiornamento* unseen and unsuspected and completely unappreciated by those who were pushing forward into the new age. His quiet and sometimes intense clinging to the mountainous wisdom of Catholicism, as he understood it, gave respectability to *everything* Catholic, for he represented in his own person the Catholic Church in the United States.

During his years of formation, he took from the Catholicism of his day, the best that it had to offer, and he made it a part of his own priesthood. That he was identified with the Catholicism of these years is not surprising, since he made it so much a part of his own self. Yet it is the substance, and not the style, of his loyalties that is important.

In his critical labors, in his innate sense of the significance of the Catholic faith, in his strong confidence in the inherent power of his religion, in his supreme loyalty to God and Christ, and in his passionate devotion to the ideals of his country, he became a strong force for good in an age when goodness was attacked fiercely and when goodness in public life was a rarity indeed.

It is a calumny and a blot on his memory to say that he associated himself with aggression and the military exploitation of the weak and helpless. He was convinced, and he was not alone in this conviction, of the justice of the American involvement in Korea and Vietnam, and it is a massive twisting of historical fact to compare the barbarism of Nazism, and the weakness of Catholic opposition to Nazi Germany to the very complex question of Vietnam. His honest conviction was that the political involvement was a just one, and he revered patriotism as the last hope for humanity. He rightly regarded his role as military vicar as a powerful tool for good, for he looked upon America's military might as the one final bulwark against a rising tide of barbarism and mass murder. He had every reason to be confident in the moral uprightness of his country's position in international affairs, for he had worked long and hard over many years with the leaders of his nation, and had helped himself to mend a broken humanity during and after World War II. If his faith in America became almost a religious conviction, it was a faith that had been built by brutal bloody experience. He was neither so unchristian nor so naïve as to think that might made right, but when he saw might fighting fiercely in the cause of right, he would give it the added strength of his own moral conviction.

In his early days, he possessed a fantastic energy, and there was a sweeping thoroughness about him that made him achieve what might be called *over-success*. But it was by dint of hard work and painstaking care, and a brilliant organizational sense that he accomplished what he did, and he was fired by a genuine priestly zeal that saw no task too small for his efforts. Everything was integrated into his priestly vision of things, and in his early years he labored in vast and varied fields. By sheer audacity of purpose and the boldness of his actions, he made himself indispensable to those for whom he labored, and he seemed to have determined very early that however critical his situation or discouraging his lot, it would bring out the best in him. This again was the fruit of a rare, rare priestly sense and the bubbly spirit that became his trademark was the acquired characteristic of a spirit that refused to be crushed or defeated.

In his early years, too, he was naturally inclined to melancholy, like most young idealists, but in the face of the huge tasks that were placed on his shoulders he acquired an optimism and a deeply rooted gaiety that melted only in the face of some biting task or decision, and this only momentarily.

I met Cardinal Spellman only twice. Once in

Alaska, when he was on his way to Christmas in Korea in 1962, and once in Tokyo in 1966, on his return from his Christmas visit to Vietnam. At our first meeting he seemed nervy and witty, held together by intense sinews of thought and feeling (it was during the first session of Vatican II), and yet vibrantly alive to all around him. He was alive with humor and a radiant amiability that was neither soft nor forced. There was a steely glint to his gaze and an unexpected toughness to his spirit. His step was feeble, but singularly independent.

At our second meeting, four years later, there was a gracious glow about him and a sparkling wit that lit up his face from time to time, as words came slowly. The fire had softened into a quiet flame and it seemed that the tiniest gust of wind would blow it out.

When the flame burned out, the whole world rose to honor his memory.

The tasks of the priesthood in the age of the *aggiornamento* are great indeed, far different from the tasks he faced, and the bold new frontiers in the Catholic apostolate are already creating a new kind of priest and a new kind of apostle. But we can find kinship with the boldness and gentle toughness of this priest whose priesthood demanded, early in his life, that he face startlingly new tasks. His wide vision of his own priestly mission can scarcely be equalled in the age of Vatican II, and the creative energy with which he labored has made an indelible mark upon this century.

## CHAPTER 5

# The Santero of San Ysidro

On the edge of the city of Santa Fe is a small village known as Agua Fria and here for many centuries have lived descendants of the early Spanish settlers who came to New Mexico after Coronado's journey north from Mexico City looking for the Seven Cities of Gold. For years it was an independent village, but in recent times it has been a small suburb of the city of Santa Fe.

The people of Agua Fria for almost a century and a half have centered their social, civic and religious lives on the small adobe church of San Ysidro, built in 1835, and the church is the focal point of every community activity. Each year they celebrate the feast of San Ysidro with great solemnity and carry in procession a *retabla* or carved wooden figure of their patron, San Ysidro, Labrador (Spanish for St. Isidore the Worker).

The *retabla* is the work of an early *santero* (religious woodcarver) whose name has been lost in history; but the tradition of the *santero* was carried on in San Ysidro by a remarkable little man whose *santos* or religious carvings are housed in several international folk art museums. He is buried in the cemetery just outside the church and he is remembered as a kind, hard-working man who left his faith emblazoned on hundreds of religious works of art.

The *santero* is part of the tradition of New Mexico and several are still alive, producing works of religious art admired by students of art all over the world. One of them, George López, carries on his craft today in Española, New Mexico, and there are several others whose works can be seen in the shops around Santa Fe and in many of the homes. But one of the most notable and most talented was Celso Gallegos, "the Santero of San Ysidro," whose nieces and nephews and cousins and countless admirers still worship in the church of San Ysidro.

When Celso Gallegos started carving *santos*, *bultos* (statues in general) and *retabla* is not known. He was doing his work as long as anyone could remember until his death in 1943, and the children of Agua Fria used to watch him as he sat in his little shed, carving figures and praying while he carved. Sometimes, they would throw small sticks and wood shavings through the door to try to distract him, but he would just smile and go on with his work. For him, the carving of *santos* was a religious action, and when they were finished, he would give them to friends. At that time, no one considered him a great artist. He was just a little man who carved wooden figures and spent a lot of time in prayer.

Celso Gallegos was born in 1864, long before the New Mexico territory was made a state. Archbishop Jean Baptiste Lamy was archbishop of Santa Fe and the rich religious traditions that had nourished New Mexicans for centuries were still very much a part of the lives of the people. Very early in his life, long before anyone now alive can remember, he became an official *Resador Velorios,* a tradition and an office that died with him. The *Resador Velorios* was one who preserved the heritage of prayers and songs that surrounded the great events of life. He sang and prayed at weddings, funerals and baptisms and handed on from one generation to the next a heritage of prayer and devotion that bound one generation to the next. Even when he was a very old man, Celso Gallegos carried out his precious office with great fidelity and devotion and he is remembered at San Ysidro for the lovely songs he sang and the prayers, rich with devotion, that he knew by heart.

There is a picture of him at the time of his marriage, before the turn of the century, in his suit that did not quite fit and with his contemplative face, mustached, with very intense eyes. He had the look of a mystic, and there seemed to be something mystical about him as he sat in his shed, behind the Church, carving and praying. He carved crucifixes, *Santos Niños* (figures of the

Christ Child), crosses for the graves of friends, San Ysidro and his ox and cart, and hundreds of figures of the saints. He would walk up and down Agua Fria carving wooden canes and saying his rosary and he could be seen in the church of San Ysidro on the great feast days, a holy man who knew more about the saints than many theologians.

In the early days of New Mexico's history, the *santero* quickly became a necessary and honored profession, but the art was lost for many years. Religious works of art in the early days were rare, and the few that reached New Mexico, like the figure of *La Conquistadora* (Our Lady of the Conquest) that graces the Cathedral of Santa Fe, were expensive and difficult to obtain. The original *santeros* began simply to copy the religious figures in the churches or in books, but soon developed a style and art of their own, and their miniature carvings of the saints are part of the great religious and cultural heritage of New Mexico.

At one time, many of Celso Gallegos' *santos* and *bultos* were enshrined in the church of San Ysidro itself, but a number of years ago priests were assigned to San Ysidro who did not understand the religious heritage of the Spanish people or the style of their religious art. Many of the *santos* looked primitive and crude and they lacked the luster and polish that the priests were accustomed to in churches. The church of San Ysidro itself was and is a simple church, with plain wooden benches and thick adobe walls, strong and simple like the faith of the people.

The *santos, bultos* and *retablas* were discarded, some of them thrown in junkpiles and in their place were put plaster-cast statues from New York. Many of the *santos* and *bultos* were masterpieces of art, treasured today by international museums and art collectors, but the priests, who were unfamiliar with the traditions of the people, looked upon them as childish attempts to imitate more sophisticated masterpieces, unworthy of the house of God. The only works of Celso Gallegos that remain in Santa Fe are in the International Folk Art Museum there, and a few pieces still cherished by old friends.

In this International Folk Art Museum in Santa Fe, there is a huge display of the work of New Mexico's *santeros,* some of them dating from 1650 and 1700, hundreds of figures, with an amazing variety of individual styles, some large, some small, some painted, some clothed, some in groups and some in simple carvings of one saint. Towards the end of the display is a glass-enclosed case with the simple inscription: *Celso Gallegos: 1864-1943.* Here are displayed some of the most notable pieces of "the Santero of San Ysidro." Hundreds have been lost, hundreds more were consigned to the junkheap after his death. Today they are priceless works of art, enshrining the faith of a simple man of faith.

Each year, at the *fiesta de San Ysidro,* in the middle of May, people talk about Celso Gallegos. They will show you his unmarked grave in the cemetery, the spot where his little workshop used to stand, and the picture of him on his wedding day which many of them have. The *fiesta* itself captures something of the spirit that inspired this *santero* and the tradition of art and beauty that he tried to carry on.

All around the Church dozens of small bonfires blaze as the people carry the *retabla* of San Ysidro around the churchyard, singing Spanish songs and shooting gun salutes to their patron. Inside the church, a choir begins the music of the solemn *Visperas,* the traditional Vesper Hour prayer honoring San Ysidro. What is very evident to one who takes part is that the heritage that nourished Celso Gallegos is still very much alive in Agua Fria, even in the eyes of the little children who share in the excitement of the feast, participating in the liturgy in a way that would edify the most exacting liturgist. It is this faith and this heritage that explains Celso Gallegos and the tradition of the *santero*. Year after year, the ancient *retabla* is a reminder of the faith that inspired this woodcarver, and as the years go on, people will dig in their attics and cellars and come up with *santos* and *bultos* that the little man carved and gave to them. Some of them will be bought by great museums and they will marvel at his artistry and superb craftsmanship. But the people of Agua Fria will remember a simple man of faith, who lived among them for seventy-nine years, and breathed beauty into pieces of wood that passed through his hands. Perhaps, someday too, the church of San Ysidro itself will come once more to be the home of his *santos* as it was the spiritual home that nourished his faith and inspired his work.

## CHAPTER 6

# Churchman of the Plains

In May, 1859, a steamer made its way up the Missouri River from St. Joseph carrying a man headed for Omaha City. Earlier in the month, he had been consecrated bishop in St. Louis and was making his way to his new assignment, the Nebraska territory. He had no cathedral, no see city, and very little money with which to start his work. Moreover, he had very little preparation for the kind of work that was suddenly thrust upon him. When James Myles O'Gorman stepped onto the docks of Omaha City 116 years ago, he opened a chapter in the history of Nebraska which has not often been told.

When Nebraskan Willa Cather wrote her novel *Death Comes for the Archbishop* she chose as her subject a pioneer Catholic bishop in New

Mexico whose history intrigued her and around whom she wove her lovely tale. Had she searched carefully the history of her own state, she might have come across the story of James Myles O'Gorman, who labored in Nebraska at the same time the subject of her novel was laboring in New Mexico.

He had a strange past. Born in County Tipperary, Ireland, he had become a Trappist at Mount Melleray in County Waterford and had gained a reputation as an able administrator. Later, when the Trappists founded a house near Dubuque, Iowa, he came with some of the first groups of monks and eventually became prior of the monastery. He would have undoubtedly remained a Trappist for the rest of his life if a papal document had not arrived at the monastery in January, 1859, appointing him vicar apostolic of the vast Nebraska territory. With great reluctance, Father O'Gorman left his monastic solitude to take on the huge labors of a pioneer bishop. He never really became acclimated to his new work and several times seriously considered returning to his monastery. His labors, however, were to leave an indelible mark on the history of religion in Nebraska.

The Omaha which greeted Bishop O'Gorman in 1859 was a sprawling, prosperous town at the crossroads of the West, where the Missouri met civilization for the first time and civilized men paused briefly in their journey across the continent. Dirt streets stretched from the river up over the hill; black trails were bordered by wooden frame buildings, restless with horses and men. There were two priests and two churches in the whole of the present state of Nebraska and the few Catholics who dotted the territory were, for the most part, poor and struggling settlers. Omaha itself had less than 5,000 inhabitants and the new bishop was not sure that it would be suitable for his see city.

But Omaha was also the Omaha of Edward Creighton who was to leave his own mark upon Nebraska and upon the Church in Nebraska. It was the gateway to the West and within a few short years hardy immigrants from Europe would be attracted to the open plains west of the city. Already, north of Omaha, a strange, visionary priest named Jeremiah Trecy had founded a colony of Irish Catholics at St. John City and soon other small communities of Polish, German and Bohemian Catholics would settle on the plains, build their churches, and plant their religious traditions in the soil of Nebraska.

The new bishop must have sensed that Omaha would be the center of a vast expansion, for he chose it for his headquarters and began a work that would keep him constantly laboring until his death fifteen years later. His spiritual jurisdiction was larger than some countries of Europe, stretching from western Missouri to the western borders of Montana and Wyoming. His flock was a mixture of white man, red man and every variety and mixture of each, and the amazing complexity of his responsibilities was baffling for one who was used to the simplicities which were inherent in the lives of those who espoused monasticism.

His collaborators, the priests who joined him in the early days, were also an odd mixture. They were scattered over hundreds of miles of pioneer country, lonely and alone in their churches, sometimes not seeing a fellow-priest for months at a time. The frontier attracted and bred strange clerical oddities, some of them unstable and temperamental, and Bishop O'Gorman had his share of these. Like Jeremiah Trecy, they came, labored and passed on to other labors elsewhere, leaving a mark and a memory. He was indebted to them for their zeal and for the communities they formed and served. He was also burdened with the instability of their ways and the uncertainty of their temperaments. At his death, he had ordained twenty priests and was slowly building up a band of devoted collaborators who would carry his work forward and stabilize his efforts.

Before his arrival in Omaha, a year before in fact, when news that a Catholic bishop might be sent to the territory reached Omaha, the city council had voted to set aside a piece of property for a bishop's residence to induce the new bishop to settle in their city. Bishop O'Gorman's decision to settle in Omaha was based, however, on other considerations and he took up residence in a house owned by a Catholic of Omaha, Thomas O'Conner, on what is now Eighth and Harney streets, not far from the present St. Frances Xavier Cabrini Church. It would be this house that would be the center of his labors for the first few years.

Later, Bishop O'Gorman would travel to the far ends of his vicariate, but his first few years were spent in stabilizing the Church in Nebraska. Very early, he brought the Sisters of Mercy to Omaha, and he envisioned the establishment of educational institutions, and the building of a cathedral. He also struggled to find funds to support his growing needs, and called upon the older Catholic communities in Germany and France to come to his assistance. He tried also to build an active Catholic community in Omaha itself and found support for his efforts from some of the early Catholic families.

Through the efforts of the Vincent Burkley family, a small choir was started and the ceremonies of the Church were carried out with fitting solemnity. Each Sunday morning a melodeon was borrowed from a local musician who had the only such instrument in the city and high Mass became a Sunday event. The melodeon eventually did double duty since it was also used by the Episcopalian Church for its services. Later, after the building of Omaha's first cathedral, a pipe organ would be shipped from the east and the cathedral would become the center of organ concerts, the first such musical events in the history of the city.

The end of the Civil War saw new developments in the Church of the Plains. The Union Pacific Railroad completed the construction of a transcontinental railroad and this brought thousands of immigrants into the new territory and made Omaha a key city in the development of the West. The Montana vicariate was separated from the Nebraska Church and Bishop O'Gorman's responsibilities were further lessened by the creation of separate ecclesiastical jurisdictions in Colorado and Utah. With the Church firmly established in the see city of Omaha and the immediate surroundings, Bishop O'Gorman made plans to travel to the far reaches of his vicariate to stabilize the Church there.

Never very robust, James Myles O'Gorman nevertheless undertook a journey of hundreds of miles to visit churches in western Nebraska and Wyoming, once the western expansion had begun. Hundreds of Irish Catholics had laid the tracks that brought the railroad west and Bishop O'Gorman followed the railroad west to visit them. He left the work of evangelizing the Indian tribes of his vicariate to men like Father Peter DeSmet, who were familiar with the problems of the Indian, and he visited Cheyenne and the growing number of small communities springing up along the path of the railroad.

When he returned to Omaha, Bishop O'Gorman turned his mind to the completion of one of the great dreams of his life: the building of a cathedral for his see city. Soon, he was sure, his vicariate would be elevated to the dignity of a diocese and he sensed that the head of the vicariate would be lacking in dignity until a cathedral graced the streets of Omaha. For two or three years, he had been collecting money along the railroad for such a purpose and a number of his priests had traveled to other parts of the country to appeal to the generosity of more prosperous

Catholic communities. Also, Edward Creighton, whose generosity to his Church had become a legend, was interested in the project. St. Philomena's Cathedral, completed in 1868, was the pride and joy of Bishop O'Gorman. It was the largest church in Nebraska and stood on Tenth and Harney streets, an impressive structure in the center of the city. The *Omaha Republican* for March 31, 1868 noted that "the solemn ceremonies of blessing and opening of the Catholic Cathedral . . . was attended by a large concourse of people . . . (and) the Catholics have now much the finest church edifice in Nebraska." Within ten years of Bishop O'Gorman's arrival in Omaha, the city had a cathedral and the Catholics of Nebraska a fitting center for their religion.

A year after the cathedral was completed, Bishop O'Gorman was required to go on a longer journey than the few hundred miles to the end of his vicariate. Several years before, in 1864, Pope Pius IX had announced the opening of an ecumenical council in Rome. The council was to open in December of 1869, and in October the Catholic bishop of Nebraska left Omaha for Europe. During his more than six-month absence, he would visit few places in Europe, because of his frail health. He took no major part in the deliberations of the council, but was able to carry on a small public relations campaign for the Church in Nebraska. When he returned to Omaha in the spring of 1870, his health was noticeably poorer.

The memory that James Myles O'Gorman left with those who knew him was the memory of a kindly, gentle priest who wove around himself an atmosphere of prayer, and who labored against almost insurmountable odds to lay the foundations for a vibrant religious community in Nebraska. With very few collaborators, he guided the Catholic community in Omaha and in the Nebraska territory, broadening his labors as the territory itself expanded. He was a contemporary of men like Edward Creighton, who themselves played decisive roles in the early history of Nebraska, and he laid the seeds for most of the Catholic institutions that would spring up on the Plains.

When he came up the Missouri River in the riverboat that brought him from St. Louis, the Catholic Church in Nebraska was only a name on a papal document. When he died in 1874, a tired and worn-out man, there was a thriving Church spread over the Plains and a cathedral to crown his fifteen years of labor. Within a few short years after his death, Creighton University would be founded and schools and hospitals would grow from the fertile seed that he planted.

At his funeral, Bishop Foley of Chicago, a fellow prelate, noted that Bishop O'Gorman had chosen to be a Trappist monk and might have lived his life in the solitude of the monastery. Instead, like the Irish monks who were his spiritual ancestors, he became a wanderer for the Lord, and almost single-handedly cut out a Church in the pioneer wilderness of Nebraska. Others, like Archbishop Jean Baptiste Lamy, whose life inspired Willa Cather's novel, were doing similar work in other parts of the United States, in those difficult pioneer years. Here, on the banks of the Missouri, James Myles O'Gorman left a testament of faith and devotion that is as much a part of pioneer history as the Pony Express, the Union Pacific Railroad, and the telegraph lines of the Western Union with which Edward Creighton spanned a continent. When he was laid to rest beneath the sanctuary of St. Philomena's Cathedral in July, 1874, an era had ended for the Church in Nebraska, an ending that was really the beginning of an important chapter in the history of Nebraska.

## CHAPTER 7

# Archbishop Lamy of Santa Fe

In the middle of the city of Santa Fe, standing like a sentinel and towering over the other buildings like a huge angel stands the Cathedral of St. Francis, a French Gothic cathedral in the middle of a Spanish-American community. The cathedral is only one more unusual landmark in this land of sharp contrasts and cultural contradictions and it is the work and achievement of one of the most unusual men in American Catholic history: Archbishop Juan Bautista Lamy, first archbishop of Santa Fe.

His very name is a contradiction. "Juan Bautista" is Spanish, but he was a Frenchman and he came to New Mexico in 1851 as vicar apostolic of the huge territory of New Mexico, recently acquired by the United States from Mexico after the

Mexican War. Before that time, New Mexico was part of the diocese of Durango, Mexico, but after its annexation by the United States, the responsibility for its spiritual administration came under the authority of the bishops of the United States. At their meeting in Baltimore in 1849, after the Mexican War, the assembled bishops wrote a request to Pope Pius IX to appoint a spiritual leader for the southwest portion of the United States and they recommended for the mammoth task a thirty-seven-year-old French priest stationed in Kentucky: Father Jean Baptiste Lamy.

The papal bull appointing him to the vicariate of New Mexico came as a complete surprise to the young Father Lamy. He accepted, however, and brought with him to Santa Fe his classmate and friend, Father Joseph Machebeuf, who was later to become the first bishop of Denver. These two men were to have a profound influence on the Catholic Church in the United States. On his arrival in New Mexico, in keeping with his new apostolic mission, Jean Baptiste became "Juan Bautista," Spanish for "John the Baptist."

After his consecration in Cincinnati, Bishop Lamy began the long journey to his see city, Santa Fe, at the other end of the American continent. He almost did not make it. The ship that carried him from New Orleans to Galveston was nearly wrecked off the Texas coast, and many of the bishop's belongings were lost, including a wagon which he had intended to use on his overland trip to Santa Fe. Later, just out of San Antonio, in the company of a U.S. Army unit going to New Mexico, he injured his ankle jumping from a wagon and had to remain behind in San Antonio for several weeks.

The Santa Fe which greeted young Bishop Lamy in 1851 was a strange mixture of Indian, Spanish and Anglo-American currents and the ecclesiastical situation in the new territory was critical. There were few priests, little clerical discipline and many of the priests were acutely sensitive to the changing political atmosphere. Many of the clergy resented the change of government and looked upon the new bishop as the political arm of the United States. The vicar-general of the city of Santa Fe, in fact, refused to accept Bishop Lamy as the lawful spiritual head of the territory and Bishop Lamy's first task was to undertake a 1,500-mile journey to Durango to obtain the official sanction of the bishop of Durango, who up to this time had been the spiritual father of New Mexico. This was easily obtained and Bishop Lamy returned to Santa Fe to begin the task of governing a vicariate larger than his native France.

Many of the native priests still refused to accept the authority of the new vicar apostolic. One of the most notorious was Father José Martínez, pastor of Taos. The priest had a large following in Taos, and when the vicar apostolic came to enforce his authority, it was necessary for his friend, Kit Carson, the great Indian scout, to provide armed men to protect the bishop from harm. Fearlessly, the young bishop proclaimed from the altar of the church of Taos his authority over the churches of New Mexico. Several priests, including the pastor of Taos, would leave the priesthood, bringing great sadness to the heart of Bishop Lamy, but the unity of the Church in New Mexico was assured by the courageous stand of the new bishop.

When Bishop Lamy began his work in New Mexico, there were only nine priests to serve over 100,000 Catholics and the territory was dotted with ancient mission churches, many of them in ruins. The mission churches were evidence of the rich spiritual heritage of the Spanish colonizers of New Mexico and of the Franciscans who had labored there for so many centuries. Even today many of these old mission churches are still standing and many others have been restored to their original condition. The religious heritage of New Mexico made a deep impression on Bishop Lamy and he was determined to extend, deepen and strengthen it by labors of his own.

He became a traveling bishop and sometimes made journeys of over 3,000 miles, covering vast deserts and climbing snow-covered mountains to reach the distant corners of his vicariate. Once his wagon train was attacked by Indians, and Bishop Lamy took a musket like the rest of the travelers and defended the wagons.

During these journeys of Bishop Lamy, Father Machebeuf remained at Santa Fe, slowly building Santa Fe as a center of religion, education and culture. Very early, the bishop brought the Sisters of Loretto to his see city to found a school and before many years had passed, the Christian Brothers would come to found a high school and college, and the Daughters of St. Vincent de Paul to found a hospital and orphanage. The bishop encouraged the bringing of the railroad to New Mexico and today the little town where the Santa Fe Railroad makes its main stop in northern New Mexico is called Lamy, after the railroad's most enthusiastic promoter.

The end of the Civil War witnessed new developments in the Church of the Southwest. Bishop Lamy's dedicated collaborator, Father Machebeuf, was made vicar apostolic of Colorado, and another confrere, Juan Salpointe, vicar apostolic of Arizona. With his own responsibilities lessened by the new appointments, Bishop Lamy turned his efforts to one of the great dreams of his life: the building of a cathedral in his see city.

His vicariate had been elevated to the rank of diocese two years after his arrival and he wanted a cathedral to grace the streets of the Royal City of Santa Fe. Architects and stonecutters came from France and the cathedral was begun. It was the pride and joy of Bishop Lamy and today his statue stands in front of the cathedral reminding visitors to Santa Fe of his dream and his achievement.

The legendary labors of Juan Bautista Lamy found a worthy chronicler in the 1920s in the novelist, Willa Cather, who came to New Mexico and was struck by the memories of Bishop Lamy that she found all over New Mexico. She wrote a novel that captured the spirit and vision of this great man and called it *Death Comes for the Archbishop*. It is the finest tribute written to the memory of this great priest and bishop.

Bishop Lamy's fine humanitarian sense became a legend in the Southwest. When the Daughters of St. Vincent de Paul came to build a hospital, the bishop gave them his own residence in which to begin their work. When there was a movement to raze a number of historical buildings in the city, including the Palace of the Governors which went back to the early days of Santa Fe, he fought for the preservation of this historical site, and today it is a fine museum housing an amazing historical record of New Mexico.

In 1885, Archbishop Lamy retired and Bishop Salpointe came from Arizona as his coadjutor and successor. After that he grew old gracefully and the people would see him from time to time at festivals and great occasions in the cathedral.

On February 13 1888, the *New Mexican* of Santa Fe, the territorial newspaper, carried the following item:

"The Most Rev. John Baptist Lamy, for nearly forty years the beloved Archbishop of Santa Fe, fell asleep in death at 7:45 in the morning. He passed away as he had lived, calmly and beautifully, a smile of Christian contentment encircling his noble face like a halo of glory."

He was seventy-four years old and had ruled the see of Santa Fe for thirty-seven years. His friend and classmate, Bishop Machebeuf, came from Denver to celebrate the funeral Mass and to deliver the sermon. Then, the great missioner and apostle of the Southwest was laid to rest before the high altar of the cathedral he had built.

## CHAPTER 8

# The Amazing Father Kino

The missionary genius of St. Francis Xavier became the inspiration for a remarkable army of missionaries in the two centuries following his death. Some of them, like Father Matteo Ricci and Robert de Nobili labored in China and India, trying to penetrate the ancient Chinese and Indian civilizations with the wisdom of Christianity. Others, like St. Isaac Jogues and St. John Brebéuf would face the fierce savagery of the North American wilderness, working with primitive Indian tribes who would ultimately destroy them. Others, like Father Eusebio Kino would become explorers and geographers, tracking down little-known peoples in the deserts of the Southwest, teaching them to plant and to pray, as they taught them to know their God and Savior.

Eusebio Kino was an Italian, born in Segno, Italy, in 1645. When he was eighteen, he was struck with a nearly fatal illness and promised that if he recovered, he would take the name of Francis, become a Jesuit, and offer himself for the missions. He seems at first to have planned to labor in the Orient, like Xavier himself, and with Father Ricci's example before him, he studied astronomy and mathematics, knowing that these studies would be of value in China. When his studies were completed, however, he was sent to the New World and arrived in Vera Cruz, Mexico, in 1681.

His first labors were more scientific than missionary. He became royal mapmaker and geographer, and accompanied an expedition of Spanish soldiers to Lower California, with the intention of following up colonization with missionary labors to the native Indian. He worked with a good measure of success and succeeded in building a mission church and in instructing the Indians in good farming techniques. His confidence in the colonizing and missionary possibilities of the California outpost was not shared by the soldiers who accompanied the expedition. Drought and danger from hostile Indians caused the abandonment of the project and Father Kino accompanied the soldiers back to Mexico City. His maps of the region which added greatly to a knowledge of Lower California were sent to Europe.

During his expedition to Lower California, Father Kino became acquainted with Guayma and Seri Indians, and he hoped to return to them to continue his missionary work among them. His assignment, however, was to that part of the Southwest known as the Pimeria Alta, inhabited by the Indians of the Pima Nation. Here, he would carry on an amazing apostolate from 1686 until his death in 1711. Besides the Pima, there were also the tribes of the Sobaipuris, the Papagos and the Yumans, each with its own dialect and each possessing distinct customs. Most of the tribes lived by primitive agricultural methods, raising maize, beans, melons and wheat for food, and cotton for clothing. Scattered over the region also were the ruins of cities and evidence of a once flourishing Indian civilization. The tribes of the Pimeria Alta were the descendants of a highly cultured people and displayed a native intelligence which Father Kino was not slow to appreciate.

In March, 1687, Father Kino reached the frontier mission outpost of Cucurpe, in the San Miguel River valley, in the shadow of the Agua Prieta Mountains. Immediately, he made plans to explore the whole territory and set up his headquarters in the Indian village of Cosari, fifteen miles inland. He named his first mission Nuestra Señora de los Dolores (Our Lady of Sorrows). He built the mission on a mesa, between two small mountain ranges, on a spot which gave a breathtaking view of the whole valley and which moreover was protected on three sides. Close by was the rushing cataract of the San Miguel River. The site chosen reveals Father Kino's scientific bent and poetic instinct, and the ruins of the mission can still be seen today. From this lovely headquarters, Father Kino would carry out his missionary labors for almost a quarter of a century.

Within ten years, Father Kino and his fellow missionaries established a chain of missions along the Altar and Magdalena Rivers. Beside the missions, or not too far distant from them, he also built ranches where orchards were planted and foods were raised, using the latest farming methods and cared for with a keen scientific eye. Father Kino became not only missioner, but manager of fruit orchards, farmlands, stock ranch and industrial plant.

His description of Mission Dolores, written in 1689, throws an interesting light on his missionary and apostolic genius: "The mission has its church adequately furnished with ornaments, chalices, bells, choir chapel, etc.; likewise a great many large and small cattle, oxen, fields, a garden with various kinds of garden crops, Castilian fruit trees, grapes, peaches, quinces, figs, pomegranates, pears and apricots. It has a forge for blacksmiths, a carpenter shop, a pack train, water mill, many kinds of grain, and provisions from rich and abundant harvests of wheat and maize, besides other things, including horses and mule herds, all of which serve and are greatly needed for the house, as well as for the expeditions and new conquests and conversions, and to purchase a few gifts and attractions with which, together with the Word of God, it is customary to contrive to win the minds and souls of the natives."

Besides, the mission and its ranches had an amazing corps of trained workers, listed enthusiastically by Father Kino: "In Dolores, besides the justices, captain, governor, *alcaldes,* fiscal mayor, *alguacil, topil* . . . masters of chapel and school, mayor domos of the house, there are . . . cowboys, ox-drivers, bakers . . . gardeners, and painters." This mission community was a compact, self-sustaining Christian community, where every art and science was cultivated for the greater glory of God and the greater good of all.

Along with this intense missionary and civilizing effort, Father Kino also became the explorer. He explored and mapped for the first time many regions of the Southwest, and followed the Colorado River to its mouth in California. He made half a dozen journeys to the Pacific coast and reached the Santa Clara Mountains in the Sierra del Pinacate, and several times traveled to the head of the Gulf of California.

Up to this time, Lower or Baja California was considered an island, and when he came to the Pimeria Alta to carry on his work, Father Kino was also convinced of this. But his many journeys of exploration, together with the information that he gathered from the Indians convinced him that it was a peninsula and that there was a land route to California. At one time, he had begun work on a boat to sail to the "California island," but once he realized that a land passage was possible, he gave up the boat project and sent the results of his investigations to his superiors in Mexico.

One of the most remarkable aspects of Father Kino's work is his combination of missionary and scientific skills, and this is shown especially by his success as a cattleman. He is in truth the first cattleman of the Southwest and the huge herds that he raised supplied food for his missions and placed his work on a firm economic foundation. As early as 1700, he headed a huge cattle drive from Mission Dolores to Bac, herding over 1,400 cattle to market, sending on several of his Indian foremen to construct corrals that would be necessary to hold the cattle once they arrived. Another time, when food was scarce at a mission in Lower California, at Salvatierra, he rounded up 700 head of cattle and sent his Indian "cowboys" on a cattle drive to the far-away mission.

Father Kino, even in his lifetime, became a legend among the Pimas. They loved him as a father, revered him as a holy man, and looked upon him as some kind of a wizard. If he had not preached to them as a representative of God, they might have considered him a god himself, and his appearance — tall, gaunt and rugged — gave him an air of something more than human. Even the toughest Indian chiefs gathered around him like children and his tiniest wish or suggestion became the concern of everyone. When the priest showed an interest in the blue shells which the Indians had brought from the coast and which indicated to Father Kino that Lower California was a peninsula, the Indians initiated a huge campaign of shell-collecting, sending scouting parties as far away as the Colorado River to gather shells of every variety.

He taught the Pimas, who were naturally peaceful and not warlike, to defend themselves against the ravaging Apache tribes which sometimes swept down through his mission territory on horse and cattle raids. Because of their ferocity, the Apaches easily blackmailed the smaller Indian villages, demanding horses and cattle in payment, and often murdering men, women and children.

Under Father Kino's leadership, the Spanish settlers were able to call upon the Pimas to protect the territory from the Apaches. Kino's presence was so important to the welfare of the district that when in 1697 Kino was ordered to return to Lower California by his superiors, the Spanish soldiers and citizens protested, declaring that Father Kino was necessary for the defense of the border territory.

In his study of Father Kino, Herbert Eugene Bolton called him "The Padre on Horseback" and his trips in the saddle show that he well deserved the title. At times, he traveled over thirty miles a day, covering huge distances and sometimes making the 1,500-mile trip from the Pimeria Alta to Mexico City. The figures taken from his diary show the following: In November, 1697, he traveled between 700 and 800 miles in thirty days; in 1698 he rode an average of twenty-five miles a day for twenty-six days; in 1699, he traveled 600 miles in thirty-five days; and in 1700, he rode over 1,000 miles in twenty-six days; in 1701, he journeyed more than 1,100 miles in thirty-two days, an average of thirty-five miles a day. And these are only the recorded trips. On his missionary tours, it was customary for Father Kino to travel at least thirty miles a day for weeks at a time. His trips brought him to his scattered missions, to unexplored territory, sometimes preaching, baptizing, taking census, distributing presents to his Indians and taking some time out for sleep. On these trips also he would supervise the butchering of cattle, the gathering of supplies, the overseeing of the orchards and crops, or some mission of mercy, such as trying to save one of his Indians from being executed by Spanish soldiers. When he was really in a hurry, as when one of his Indians was in trouble, he was known to have ridden more than seventy-five miles in one day. This amazing ubiquity made him even more of a marvel in the eyes of the Indians. Father Kino died in 1711, at Magdalena, one of his missions. He was almost sixty-seven years old at the time of his death. He had traveled to Magdalena to dedicate a chapel to St. Francis Xavier, to whom he was especially devoted and fell sick during the dedication Mass. His deathbed consisted of a mattress of calf-skins, Indian blankets and a pack-saddle for a pillow. Everything he ever possessed he gave away, and so he died with nothing but the bed upon which he was resting.

In his biography of Father Kino, Herbert Eugene Bolton applied to his words what had been written about another great missionary, Father Las Casas, the great Protector of the Indians: "In contemplating such a life, all words of eulogy seem weak and frivolous. The historian can only bow in reverent awe before ... (such) a figure. When now and then in the course of centuries God's providence brings such a life into this world, the memory of it must be cherished by mankind as one of its most precious and sacred possessions. For the thoughts, the words and the deeds of such a man, there is no death. The sphere of their influence goes on widening forever. They bud, they blossom, they bear fruit, from age to age."

In Eusebio Francis Kino, missionary, explorer, rancher, geographer, historian, is seen a multi-faceted genius whose missionary labors covered thousands of miles, planting the faith among primitive Indian tribes and civilizing them in the process. That he is not better known is due to the fact that he was a self-effacing man whose only memorial was in the hearts of his beloved Indians. Somewhere in the vast Southwest where he labored, his body is buried, but no one knows where. All that remains is the distant memory of the Padre on Horseback, the missionary-frontiersman, whose life reads like an old Spanish legend. Like the cowboys who would come after him he rode tall in the saddle, and is rightly considered by historians a key figure in the history of the Southwest and a remarkable missionary worthy of the race of his patron, St. Francis Xavier.

## CHAPTER 9

# The Martyrs of Nagasaki

High on a hill in the middle of Nagasaki, not too far from the epicenter of the atomic bomb explosion of 1945, stands an unusual chapel with its double, odd-looking spire dominating the landscape. This is the chapel of San Felipe, and the spot commemorates the execution of twenty-six Japanese martyrs in the year 1597, when Catholicism was scarcely fifty years old in the Japanese isles.

This event, however, was just the beginning, and before fifty more years had passed, Japan was rocked with a wave of persecution rivaling in its ferocity and inhumanity the Spanish Inquisition which at this time was at its height in Europe. Eventually, Japanese Catholics were forced underground and Christianity disappeared from the

Japanese scene for over 200 years, reappearing when the Emperor Meiji opened Japan to the West in the middle of the nineteenth century. At that time, Japanese Catholics came out of hiding, and the story of their amazing preservation of their faith for over two centuries without priests touched the heart of the pope himself and brought about the canonization of the first martyrs, the heroic twenty-six who were crucified outside the city of Nagasaki, on this lone hill which today is almost in the center of the city.

In many ways, some view the martyrdom as being unnecessary. The Society of Jesus had sent missionaries to Japan on the heels of St. Francis Xavier's hurried apostolate in that country. The first Jesuit superior, Father Alessandro Valignano, was a missionary genius, whose spirit and tactics inspired the great Matteo Ricci himself, the great Jesuit missionary to China. Valignano realized that here was a rich harvest for the Catholic faith and for Christ, but that here was by no means a rich harvest for the Spanish colonizers. The Spanish and Portuguese at this time were the great explorers of the Far East. Goa had become Portuguese and the Philippines were already Spain's. Both looked with greedy eyes to Japan and to China, but these two great nations, recognizing the colonizing designs of the European merchantmen, severely limited access to their countries. Through Valignano's superb gift for human relations, the Jesuits were permitted to evangelize Japan, with the firm understanding that their efforts were not to provide a doorway for the coming of the "southern barbarians," as the Europeans were called. For the sake of their work, the Jesuits had to make concessions to the Japanese rulers, even to the point of acting as agents of the Japanese government in its silk-trading enterprises.

The unity of the Japanese missionary work was the strongest factor in the spread of the Catholic faith in Japan, but that work was not without its critics. Chief among these were the Franciscan friars, who had come to the Philippines in the wake of the Spanish colonization there. They were not silent in their criticism of Jesuit missionary policies and determined at the first opportunity to add another dimension to the missionary work in Japan. They arrived in Kyoto about 1593, and carried on works of mercy and charity which were to be remembered for centuries. Their horror for paganism, however, and their complete lack of understanding of the Japanese situation brought them into frequent conflict with the Japanese authorities and it took only one major incident to whip the fury of the Japanese *shoguns* (military governors) to the white heat of persecution. That incident was the unfortunate "*San Felipe* Affair" which triggered the persecution that would eventually destroy Christianity in Japan.

The *San Felipe* was a Spanish ship, loaded down with rich cargo, bound for Mexico. Battered by a typhoon, it limped into the port of Urado, on the island of Shikoku. The Japanese *shogun*, Hideyoshi, who tolerated Christianity only because of his admiration for Valignano, immediately seized the ship. This brought on the anger and rage of the Spanish captain and his crew, who appealed to the Franciscans for help in saving the ship and its cargo. The intercession of the friars only infuriated Hideyoshi, who at this time was trying to unite Japan under one ruler and had recently fought an exhausting war in Korea. He was persuaded that Christian missionaries were part of a plot to colonize Japan and he accused the missionaries of being agents of a foreign power, paving the way for the conquest of the Japanese islands by the Western nations. His fears were not entirely unfounded, for he had only to look at Goa, the Philippines and the New World, where the missionary effort was so closely associated with the conquest of the native peoples. In a burst of fury, the Japanese *shogun* ordered the arrest and execution of all missionaries and Christians. Friends of the missionaries interceded and the number of those arrested was small in comparison with the number of Christians in Japan. Among those arrested were Philip of Jesus, a Mexican Franciscan friar; Paul Miki, a Jesuit scholastic; and several prominent Christians from Kyoto and Osaka, including two young boys, ages twelve and thirteen.

The execution was scheduled to take place in Nagasaki, the Christian center of Japan, undoubtedly as a warning to all Japanese Christians. The prisoners were to be marched from Osaka to the place of execution, several hundred miles away. Before their terrible journey began, their ears were cut off, and they were loaded on oxcarts and driven through the streets of Osaka. The execution and martyrdom took place on a hill called Nishizaka, overlooking Nagasaki Bay, close to a little highway that led into the city. Here, crosses were erected and with hundreds of people watching, the martyrs were bound to the crosses, pierced through the abdomen and heart, and left to die. There were twenty-six of them, the oldest a sixty-four-year-old man, the youngest a twelve-year-old boy.

For centuries, the martyrdom was commemorated by a huge stone and twenty-six beautiful trees. But in 1962, an unusual chapel, a museum and a huge sculpture by the Japanese artist Yasutake Funakoshi were completed, a fitting memorial to the heroic martyrdom of this amazing band of Japanese Christians. The memory of their ordeal strengthened and supported other Japanese Christians during the terrible years that followed, when the faith was driven from the islands, and the Christian Church became an underground Church. The martyrdom was but the beginning of a massive persecution, one of the most barbaric in the whole history of Christianity.

Today, the fairy-like spires of the chapel of San Felipe of Jesus mark the spot of the martyrdom and the impressive monument of Yasutake Funakoshi bears witness to the heroic spirit and unconquerable faith of these twenty-six men. Jesuit Fathers from several countries are custodians of the shrine and they recount for the visitor the historic events that took place there. The museum houses a rare collection of letters, manuscripts and other historical items dating from the time of the martyrdom, including several letters of St. Francis Xavier himself. In historic Nagasaki, the scene of so many monumental events in Japanese history, the Shrine of the Twenty-Six Martyrs links Japanese Catholicism with its memorable past and holds up a shining light of faith and courage to light the way into the future.

# CHAPTER 10

# Francisco de Vitoria: Father of International Law

The University of Salamanca in Spain in the sixteenth century was the theological center of Europe. It was from this university that the great theologians were to come who would shape the decrees of the Council of Trent in the middle of this century, and it was from this university that one of the great moralists of the Catholic Church was to come. His name was Fray Francisco de Vitoria, a Dominican friar, and he is famous for two singular achievements: opposition to the colonial policies of the Spanish Crown, and laying the basis for international law, and, eventually the establishment of a world body like the United Nations.

It was the colonial policies of the Spanish Crown that first caused this quiet teacher of theology to speak out. In the wake of her New World conquests, Spain had subdued the native Indian tribes, often enslaving them, and, in the name of Christianity, robbing them of their rights. The first voice to be raised was that of Fray Bartholomew de las Casas, who made at least seven trips from the West Indies to Spain to protest the enslavement of the Indian. He pleaded for compassion, a sense of justice and a respect for the human dignity of the Indian.

Las Casas' efforts brought about minor reforms. A commission of theologians and jurists was formed to study the matter, and all without exception held that the Indians were the rightful owners of the lands of New Spain and that it was sinful, unchristian and immoral to rob them of their lands. The immense riches that came in the wake of the Spanish conquests had turned the heads of many of the Spanish conquistadors and, in their greed, they disregarded the rights of the native Indian. When these matters were brought to the attention of Vitoria, who was considered Spain's master theologian, he wrote: "The events in the Indies . . . make my blood run cold." The fact that many of these things were done in the name of Christianity by those who professed the Catholic faith made him even more disturbed, and so he turned his mind to study these things more thoroughly.

As he started to speak out, there were those who told him that he was interfering in matters which were none of his business, that he was questioning the legitimate authority of the Spanish Crown in these matters, and that the pope himself had authorized the Spanish conquerors to act in this manner. This appeal to papal authority for acts that were obviously motivated by greed and a lust for power moved Vitoria to put his thoughts into writing, and there appeared his definitive study of the matter called simply *De Indis: The Affair of the Indies.*

"Insofar as I am able," Vitoria wrote, "I avoid quarreling with these people. But if, in the end, I am absolutely compelled to give an unequivocal answer, I shall state my true opinion." His answer rocked the whole Spanish nation.

The actions of the Spanish nation, he said, in subduing the Indian, were unchristian, immoral and unjust, contrary to every law of human decency, and contrary to every principle of the Christian faith. Thou shalt not steal, he said, thou shalt not kill, applies to nations as well as men, and the Spaniard had no more right to steal from an Indian than an Indian did to steal from a Spaniard. In his answer, Vitoria states the basic principles of the natural law, upon which many principles of Catholic morality are based. Finally, when someone objected that the pagan Indian hindered the progress of the Catholic faith in New Spain, Vitoria bluntly answered: "I have not seen that the Catholic faith has been preached to these people in such a way that they could accept it reasonably." In any case, their human rights could not be disregarded in the name of the faith.

The king of Spain, Charles, was angered at Vitoria's outspoken criticism of his government's policies, and wrote a letter to Vitoria's Dominican superior insisting that the Dominican cease his writings, and that anything that he should write in the future should be cleared by the Spanish Crown. To this Vitoria respectfully but firmly replied that he "served only God and truth" and that the king could well direct his anger at the abuses themselves, since they were perpetrated by those who claimed to represent the highest authority of the land, the king himself.

What Vitoria laid down in his study of the Indian question was a single moral standard applicable to all men and to governments and individuals alike. Much of Europe had been strongly influenced by the writings of Niccolo Machiavelli, an Italian renaissance writer who had stated in his book *The Prince* that a king was above the moral law, and that he had to use treachery, deceit and any means necessary, moral or immoral, to extend his power. He stated boldly that a king is superior to law and morality, and that no moral or religious considerations could hamper his power, and that he could use any means, including murder, to advance his power and safeguard his rule. Vitoria struck out with every insight of Christian wisdom and every tenet of the Catholic faith to combat this concept of the Christian ruler, and he called the Spanish Crown and the Spanish colonists back to a sense of justice and decency based upon their Catholic heritage.

He did not altogether succeed, but in facing the Indian problem, he at the same time developed a concept of international law, based upon those common laws of decency and justice which should regulate the relations of one people with another, or one nation with another. Recognizing that the conquest of the native Indian involved a theory of war, he developed his thinking into what is considered the classic study of the problem of war, his treatise on *The Law of War*.

Most of the nations of Europe at the time were concerned only about their own national self-interest; anything was considered moral if it furthered the interests of the nation itself. There was no law governing the relations of one nation with another, or one people with another, and Machiavelli's principles seemed eminently suited to the progress of each individual nation. Vitoria appealed to the natural law, and stated that this law had been engraved upon human nature itself, and that to transgress it was to transgress the very law of God who had imprinted it on the heart of man.

With regard to war and conquest, Vitoria had this to say: "Difference of religion is not a just cause for war. Neither is the extension of empire, or the personal glory of the ruler, far less the profit to be gained from conquest, or some other advantage to the State. Only the gravest reasons of national well-being and security, justify war, since the evils that come from war are so severe and destructive."

Through a series of painstaking questions, Vitoria examines the whole morality and theology of war, laying down the basic principle that justice and justice alone should regulate the relations of nations with each other. Wars, or conquest, he said, which are based upon national self-interest or the mere expansion of empire were immoral and unchristian, and that ruler who engaged in them could expect the severest judgment of God when he stood before Christ to make a detailed account of all he did during his earthly tenure.

His words were not received very kindly at the Spanish court, but the eminence of his authority, and the obvious solidity of his teaching, brought about changes in colonial policy and brought into focus for the first time in history a concept of a "Law of Nations," as Vitoria called it, the moral law as applied to international relations. Four centuries later, the principles he enunciated would be used as the basis, first of the League of Nations, and then of the United Nations. Vitoria deserves, in very truth, to be called the Father and Founder of International Law, and he is considered such by a vast number of authorities in the field of law.

The world situation in the wake of Columbus' discovery of the New World had required a new application of Christian moral principles. Vast new lands had been opened up, offering immense riches to nations and individuals. These lands were inhabited by millions of natives who had never been exposed to the Catholic faith. Catholic moralists had never faced this kind of situation before, and many were reluctant to examine the moral structure of this new situation. Francisco de Vitoria realized that it had to be done, and he took the initiative to see to it that it was.

As one writer has written of him: "Vitoria saw that theology, and especially moral theology, could no longer remain separated from current affairs, from the actions of men and nations. He knew that moral theology to be vital must be applied to individual cases; otherwise, it would lose all its force and become only a consideration of opinions. So, far from staying in the clouds, he turned his mind more and more to current problems. As a result, he surpassed his contemporaries in the knowledge of world affairs, and became the prime internationalist of his day."

When the United States Department of Justice, several years ago, commissioned the artist, Boardman Robinson, to paint murals for the foyer of its buildings in Washington, D.C., one of the subjects chosen for the mural was Francisco de Vitoria. Through the studies of Dr. James Brown Scott, one-time professor of international law at Georgetown University, and secretary of the Carnegie Endowment for International Peace, Vitoria's place in the history of law was recognized by leading world authorities. In 1946, at an international convocation honoring Vitoria on the fourth centenary of his death, Dr. Scott was invited to give a lecture for the occasion at the Dominican Convent of San Esteban in Salamanca, where the Dominican friar had lived during his teaching years. This was in the midst of the Nuremburg trials, following World War II, where principles of international law were applied to the Nazi war crimes. Just the year before, at San Francisco, the foundations of a tribunal of international law had been laid by the establishment of the United Nations.

Thus, one small Dominican friar, deeply imbued with a sense of justice from his intimate knowledge of Catholic teaching, almost single-handedly changed the policies of the Spanish conquistadors, and in doing so, laid the foundations for a development in world affairs four centuries later. It is notable also that most of his disciples were among those theologians who helped rebuild Catholicism after the Reformation when the Catholic Church called the Council of Trent, almost on the date of Vitoria's death in 1546. He died before he saw the full result of his labors, consulted by the very king who had been angered by his outspoken writings.

Because of his labors, Franciscan friars would be able, in later years, to freely spread the Gospel among the Indians of New Mexico and California, and Father Francisco Kino would be able to do his amazing work among the Indians of northern Mexico and Arizona. The Jesuits, too, would be able to establish their remarkable reductions in Paraguay, where the Indians lived in a social paradise unparalleled in the history of colonization. Francisco de Vitoria enunciated a whole new missionary concept, and turned the tide of a cruel exploitation that might have destroyed the Indian before he had even come to know the blessings of the Christian faith.

In living up to his commission as theologian and moralist, Vitoria fulfilled one of the highest missions given to a man, the mission of a teacher of divine truth. In remaining faithful to that commission, in the face of great difficulty and danger to himself, he brought blessings to untold millions and laid the seeds for a charter of freedom and justice that is being realized in our own time and century.

## CHAPTER 11

# The Carthusian Martyrs of England

The Carthusian Order is not very well known in the United States, even though there has been a monastery of the Order in this country for over twenty years. It is a very ancient Order, dating back to St. Bruno of Cologne, who began living a simple contemplative life in the wilds of Grenoble about 1080. Later, he was called to be the personal adviser of Pope Urban II, and he left a small group of monks in Grenoble, at a place called La Grande Chartreuse, who would carry on his way of life and eventually extend it throughout Europe.

The Carthusian life is a blend of community monastic life and that of the hermit. It is a strict, austere life, totally contemplative, and is the only monastic order in the Church that has never needed reform. Even today, it has lessened none of its austerity, and its members are silent and unknown, living out their lives of penance and prayer in complete seclusion.

During the reign of Henry VIII in England, there was a flourishing "Charterhouse" in London, famous for the quiet holy lives that were lived there. It stood on the edge of the city, its orchards and gardens spreading out towards the Tudor mansions of the period. Carthusian life in England had flourished for over three centuries, ever since the days of England's most famous Carthusian, St. Hugh of Lincoln, who had crossed wits with King Henry II, in the late twelfth century. Hugh, reluctantly, had been made bishop of Lincoln, but he remained a Carthusian at heart and his example drew many candidates into the Carthusian cloister.

Thomas More in his early days spent four years in residence at the London Charterhouse and was strongly attracted to the silent life of the Carthusians. On the advice of his spiritual director, however, he chose another vocation, but would join his spiritual brothers in martyrdom. He would even watch them go to their martyrdom from his cell in the Tower of London, remarking to his daughter Meg that God was delaying his own martyrdom because his had been a softer life than theirs. Certainly, much of the spirit shown by St. Thomas More in his life and in his death he acquired in the silent years when he made the London Charterhouse his home.

The spiritual ideal exemplified by the London Carthusians drew many sons of London's finest families into the Carthusian cloister. Its solemn liturgy and obvious austerity contrasted sharply with the whirl and glitter and sometimes open immorality of the court of Henry VIII. In 1531, just on the eve of the violent persecution inaugurated by Henry VIII over his marriage to Anne Boleyn, a remarkable man was elected prior of the London Charterhouse, a man who would lead his community to martyrdom on the scaffold at Tyburn, thereby writing one of the saddest and most touching pages in English religious history.

John Houghton, the prior, was from Essex, and had studied law at Cambridge before entering the Carthusian life in 1515. He had a deep love for Carthusian life, and was a gentle, kindly prior, who guided firmly his monastic community and became the spiritual father of a whole generation of young Carthusians. He possessed the gentleness and the strength of personality which is characteristic of the English saints, from St. Cuthbert to St. Thomas More. Kind and genial, he nevertheless had the tenacity and the strength of spirit in a crisis of faith worthy of St. Thomas a Becket, who died by the hand of another king in another age. That Blessed John Houghton's teaching and training was solid and thorough is proved by his community following him to a painful and terrible martyrdom.

When the young Houghton entered the Carthusian cloister in 1515, the quiet tranquil life there gave no indication that it would not go on forever, but that quiet life was abruptly interrupted in the spring of 1534, when the English parliament, on orders from the king himself, passed the Act of Succession. This act was the first in a series of acts of parliament aimed at legalizing Henry's marriage to Anne Boleyn, dissolving his marriage with Catherine of Aragon, assuring the succession of any son born to Anne, eventually making the king supreme head of the Church in England.

The Act of Succession appeared harmless enough, and there were many whose conscience could accept it. In its strictly legal terminology, it was a strictly legal matter and did not involve matters of faith. Even Thomas More admitted that parliament was quite free to make anyone the king's successor and if this had been the substance of the act, Thomas More would have accepted it. The preamble to the act, however, implied more, and both Thomas More and Bishop John Fisher read the true intent of the act: the denial of the supreme authority of the pope.

The prior of the Carthusians was not unaware of the events that led up to the act, and when the king's commissioners appeared at the doors of the monastery demanding that the monks take an oath accepting the Act of Succession, Houghton saw in the oath an implicit denial of the king's marriage to Catherine. What the king wanted to do, the prior told the commissioners, was his own business, but he demanded that his monks be left in peace. When the commissioners, under orders from Thomas Cromwell, insisted that he and his community take the oath, the prior refused and he and his procurator were taken into custody.

Their arrest caused much consternation in

England, and the king, eager not to give the impression of religious persecution, was also disturbed, although he insisted that even the religious of his kingdom take the oath. Edward Lee, the archbishop of York visited the Carthusians in prison, and persuaded them that the faith was not at stake, and that this was purely a legal matter. John Houghton was not sure, but he was quite willing to defer to the judgment of an archbishop, if it meant that the Carthusians would be left alone. There is a good chance that he never saw the actual text of the act, where the authority of the pope is implicitly denied. The prior agreed to take the oath, and he and his procurator were permitted to return home.

His community, however, was not happy with his decision and most of them would not agree to take the oath. They felt that their action would give approval to the king's divorce from his lawful wife, and their conscience would not permit this. Houghton pointed out that the act involved only the succession itself and that this was a legal matter. After much reluctance, and in the presence of the armed soldiers of the king, the monks took the oath.

Houghton's concern, of course, was not to become involved in merely legal matters, and to preserve the religious life of his community, if a matter of conscience was not at stake. He was sure, however, that the Carthusians had not seen the end of harassment, and his fears were well-grounded. Soon after their first encounter with Henry's commissioners, parliament passed another act, the Treason Act, sometimes called the Act of Supremacy. According to this act, it was high treason not to acknowledge that King Henry was the supreme head of the Church in England. One by one religious houses were visited by the king's commissioners and John Houghton saw the handwriting on the wall. Calling his community together, as other religious were arrested and imprisoned, he told them his fears, and suggested that they prepare for the ordeal ahead. Each monk made a general confession, making his peace with God; then he made his peace with his Carthusian brothers, begging forgiveness for any failings in charity; then the whole community took part in a Mass of the Holy Spirit, asking for God's guidance.

Strengthened in this way, John Houghton put aside the simplicity of the dove and decided to use the cunning of the serpent. He asked for an interview with Thomas Cromwell and boldly demanded that his monks be exempt from the obligation of the act. Deep in his heart, he was convinced that the king would not dare to lay hands on consecrated religious, but he was mistaken. His request was denied and a few days later, he and several of his fellow Carthusians were once more imprisoned in the Tower of London.

In their interrogation before Cromwell, they expressed their willingness to consent to the king's wishes "insofar as the law of God might allow," but Cromwell refused this qualification. Like Thomas More, they were concerned that they would not unwittingly be responsible for their own martyrdom, and they were quite willing to leave legal matters to the lawyers. When Cromwell demanded that they swear to the oath without qualifications, they absolutely refused, and made it clear that for them a matter of divine faith was at stake.

Their trial took place in Westminster Hall on April 28th and 29th of the year 1535. In his usual manner, Cromwell bullied a very reluctant jury into pronouncing a verdict of guilty. As they left the Tower for Tyburn on May 4th, they did not know that they were being watched by Thomas More from his cell window, and the peace and joy on their faces gave him added strength to endure his own ordeal.

King Henry showed his "mercy" to the monks by permitting them to be executed in their monastic habits. Houghton embraced his executioner before the death blows were struck, and he was fully conscious as the executioner hacked away at his body, his death being delayed by the thickness of his monastic robes. Invoking the name of Christ, he died, the whole of England shocked at the barbarism of their king.

The rest of the Carthusian community were again given the chance to save their lives, and upon their refusal to take the oath, they were tried and sent to their deaths. The final group was imprisoned, chained and systematically starved, each member's misery relieved somewhat by the secret devotion of Margaret Gigs, the adopted daughter of St. Thomas More. She bribed her way into their prison, acting as a milkmaid, and placed food between the lips of the starving men. She brought clean linen and washed them and even when forbidden to continue her work of mercy, she climbed onto the roof of the prison and lowered food to them. The men of God died in chains, God accepting their total consecration to Him in a way that demanded the last full measure of sacrifice.

As Dom David Knowles has written of them: "Rarely indeed in the annals of the Church have any confessors of the faith endured trials longer, more varied or more bitter than these unknown monks. They had left the world, as they hoped, for good; but the children of the world, to gain their private ends, had violated their solitude to demand of them an approval and a submission which they could not give. They had long made of their austere and exacting rule a means to the loving and joyful service of God; pain and desolation, therefore, when they came, held no terrors for them. When bishops and theologians faltered or denied, they were not ashamed to confess the Son of Man. They died faithful witnesses to the Catholic teaching that Christ had built his Church upon a rock."

Unlike Thomas More, their names are scarcely known to Catholics, but like him they resemble their Master by their sufferings and their martyrdom. In all, seventeen Carthusians went to their deaths. They had vowed themselves to a contemplative life in order to imitate Christ in His hidden life; by a strange decree of divine Providence, they were destined to imitate Him in His sufferings and crucifixion.

## CHAPTER 12

# The Emergence of St. Thomas Aquinas

In the summer of 1256, the thirty-one-year-old Thomas Aquinas stepped into the pulpit of the Church of St. Genevieve in Paris to deliver the inaugural address opening his tenure of office as professor at the University of Paris. From his audience was noticeably absent his fellow-professors and several colleges of the university. The lecture of the young Dominican was the climax of a conflict three decades old between the mendicant friars who were opening new frontiers in the Catholic apostolate and the secular masters of the university who saw in the zeal, energy and boldness of the friars a threat to their good name and to their very existence.

    The students who had gathered for the past four years at the Dominican Convent of St.

Jacques were there, in their colorful garb and fighting spirit, for Thomas had become for them a symbol of an exciting new adventure in knowledge. Like his master, the encyclopedic Albertus Magnus, Thomas sparked the intellect, made daring new judgments on the issues of the age and even dipped his mind and his pen into the forbidden world of Aristotle and the Arabian philosophers.

When Thomas Aquinas rose to speak, and his thunderous voice boomed through the interior of the church, he had come to the apex of his career, and in his address summed up in lucid Latin the significance of his thought and labors. The Dominicans had recovered a concept of the Christian teacher lost for centuries and the brilliant leadership of their founder, Dominic of Calereuga, had stamped upon their work an idealism that drew into their Order the best minds and the best men of the century. The young Dominican's carefully chosen text captured his own concept of his work and the program which the Dominicans were to follow for at least another two centuries: "You have watered the hills from Your upper rooms, the earth will be filled with the fruit of Your work."

Thomas' reception into the faculty of the University of Paris was not merely his own private achievement, but had been prepared for by the labors of Johannus Teutonicus, the dynamic superior general of the Order who had succeeded to the labors of St. Dominic. He had mapped out the objectives of the Order of Preachers, and paramount in those objectives was the education of Thomas Aquinas whom he had discovered at the University of Naples and brought to Paris. He had commissioned Albertus Magnus, the greatest mind of the age, to create and direct a *studium generale* at Cologne and there the best minds of the Dominican Order had been sent, Thomas Aquinas among them. After four years at Cologne, and seven with Albertus, the young Aquinas began his teaching career at Paris, and in the face of the violent opposition of the secular masters, by order of the pope himself, was received into the faculty of the university. This triumph was an end and a beginning: an end to one era of Catholicism and the beginning of another.

The doctorate, which admitted him to the ranks of the university professors, was conferred upon him in the palace of the archbishop of Paris and was attended by the whole university faculty. The inaugural address of a confrere was usually attended by the whole faculty also, but since Thomas Aquinas had been received against the will of the professors themselves and in direct opposition to their expressed wishes, his fellow-professors did not hear the opening remarks of the mendicant friar.

Those who listened were his own Dominican brethren, the students who were being shaped by his new vision of man and human knowledge, and the papal molders of policy at Rome.

"As the mists and waters fall upon high mountains, unite, and break and tumble through a thousand rents and fissures, working their way down, forcing their way on, till they reach the broad plain, clothing it with fruitfulness, nourishing the wildlife there, sprouting tree and grain and flowers, so the stream of Truth, blending with man's mind and substance, clothes him with strength and dignity."

This invitation to intellectual excellence was not lost upon the hearers, and it was this very invitation, proclaimed more by example than by word, that had drawn up the secular professors, almost to a man, in opposition to the mendicants. The closed society of the professional educator had been invaded by apostles and prophets for whom truth was a noble work and the proclamation of truth a consecrated mission. The defection of such brilliant masters as Alexander of Hales and John of St. Gilles into the mendicant orders had made the conflict even more bitter. During the master-generalship of Jordan of Saxony, the Order of Preachers had filled its quiver with the best minds of the universities, and Thomas' reception of the doctorate was the crowning blow in a bitter battle that would be waged in the presence of the pope himself.

When the inaugural address was ended, Thomas Aquinas was invested with the insignia of his office. The doctor's ring was placed upon his finger, symbolically wedding him to Truth, and he was given "power to teach over all nations." The robes and the cap of the doctor, making him part of the greatest university in the world, was bestowed, and he was told that he could from that day forward "be seated among the Doctors."

His inaugural address had been both a charter and a battle cry and as such it was understood. The text of his address was rushed to a villa outside Paris where a university professor named William of St. Amour was preparing a work of his own. A year later, Thomas Aquinas and Bonaventure, the Franciscan, would both battle the content and the ideas of William's piece of writing. But now both of them, Bonaventure having joined Thomas on St. Genevieve's Hill, received the congratulations of their fellow-friars after the ceremonies and solemnities of the day. For Thomas Aquinas, an era of preparation was ended; for the Church and for the world, an era was begun.

## The Aquino Family

The Aquinos were vassals of the emperor, Frederick II, and lived on the site of a castle stolen from the abbey of Monte Cassino over 200 years before Thomas' birth. The town of Aquino, from which the family got its name, was in the center of the Campagna Felice in the ancient Terra de Lavora, near Naples. The plain was surrounded by mountains and on one of them, bare and bleak as it breaks the horizon, the Aquinos had built their castle on the ruins of the one once owned by the abbey of Monte Cassino. It was called Rocca Sicca and was the home of Landulf, count of Loreto and Belcastro; Theodora, of the noble house of Caraccioli, and their four sons and two daughters. They were a family dedicated to arms and the three older sons, Aimo, Landulf and Raynoldo, were soldiers in the army of Frederick II, together with their father.

Landulf belonged to the house of Sommacoli, one of the most remarkable families in middle Italy. His father, Thomas, for whom the young Aquino was named, was lieutenant-general of the Holy Roman Empire, and his mother, Frances of Suabia, was a sister of the emperor. Thomas Aquinas was thus a second cousin of the emperor, Frederick II.

Since the Aquino family served the emperor, the sons of Aquino became soldiers and were trained from boyhood for the profession of arms. The older brother, Landulf, named after his father, was known as a soldier of some skill, and the younger brother, Raynoldo, besides his military ability, was an accomplished poet, and a fond admirer of the courts of love of Provence and southern France. This brother was to come to a tragic end, for after falling out of favor with the emperor, Frederick II, he was beheaded. The Aquinos had long held the land in the Campagna Felice, and their men and mercenaries were at the disposal of the emperor in his many wars with the popes, and in the odd and strange career that brought him from Germany to Jerusalem, from his intellectual stronghold in the University of Naples to his harems in Sicily. The Aquinos were soldiers and they saw little beyond the profession of the soldier and the glory of the Aquinos.

Theodora D'Aquino had brought with her in marriage to Landulf, lands and titles of her own. She was a proud, strong-willed woman who ruled her family and her sons with a strength and determination not unlike that of Eleanor of Aquitaine. In the Aquino family, she was the dominant personality and after the death of her husband in 1242, she ruled the destiny of the Aquino family with an iron hand.

What motivated the decision to place Thomas Aquinas in the care of the Benedictine monks at Monte Cassino, is not known. In 1230, when the young boy entered the famous abbey, the battle between Frederick II and the aged pope, Gregory IX, was at its height and the family may have feared for the safety of one so young at the castle of Rocca Sicca. He was five years old at the time and the abbot of Monte Cassino was Sinnebald, a distant relative of the Aquinos. It could well be that even at this early date, the family had decided to send one of their sons to the imperial university at Naples, founded in the very year of Thomas' birth. It was a favorite project of the emperor and an education at Monte Cassino would prepare Thomas well for a university career.

At five years of age, the young boy left the family circle and became a student of the Benedictines. He was to stay with them for almost ten years and the impress of these years of solitude and contemplative life was to leave a deep mark upon the personality of Thomas Aquinas that would never be eradicated, neither by the passage of time nor by human design.

## The Benedictine Experience

The homelife of the Aquinos had little influence on Thomas Aquinas. He touches his family only at that point where his Dominican vocation brings him into conflict with them. For all practical purposes — educationally, socially and psychologically — the Benedictine Abbey of Monte Cassino was his family.

He certainly did not enter into the politics of the age or take part in the struggle between emperor and pope which rocked those years, even though this struggle would eventually drive him from the cloister. What influenced him was the rhythm of monastic life, the contemplative outlook it fostered and the atmosphere set up by solitude, liturgy and sacred study.

Since he entered at the early age of five, there was no other influence in his tender years, and preoccupation with truth, which was to occupy his whole life, began when he chanted the psalms of David, listened to the reading of the scripture from the masterly Latin Vulgate, and began the steps of that broad intellectual discipline embodied in the *Trivium* and *Quadrivium*, the backbone of medieval education.

The Benedictine tradition that nourished him was already ancient, going back to St. Benedict of Nursia, seven centuries before. It was not directed to action or to the world outside the cloister, even though it often produced men who became practical men of affairs. It was geared essentially to eternity, to preparing man for the beatific vision, the final goal of human life, and to directing life with strength and simplicity to God and God alone. It was primarily neither a sedentary existence nor a moral revolt from "the world," but was intensely and passionately contemplative, in an age when the highest value was placed upon God and the personal pursuit of an eternal destiny.

Thomas Aquinas always possessed the tranquil stability acquired in his Benedictine years. Not only that but in the lecture halls and libraries of the great abbey, his mind came into contact with the great minds of the past and he always found it easy to bridge the gap of years and make a man his contemporary. The profound theological vision which permeates his whole thought was also acquired in these years and this is the most critical quality acquired in his Benedictine years. This theological vision was to be the unifying force of his whole genius, making him at once vibrant of intellect and deeply wrapped in prayer. When he was violently wrenched from Monte Cassino at the age of fourteen, he was thrown back into family life from which he had been cut off from the age of five. He was not long in rejecting the involvement in politics and war that was the whole existence of the Aquinos and this rejection would bring upon him some of the bitterest suffering of his whole life. His family never understood the tenacity with which he clung to his chosen vocation, as they never forgave him for choosing the Dominicans who, in the battle between pope and emperor, were firm in their loyalty to the pope. Thomas' tenacity was the fruit of his

Benedictine experience and when his hour came to die, he asked once more to join the company of those who had been the companions of his early years.

### Pope and Emperor

In 1239, Monte Cassino became a besieged fortress. In the spring of that year, the pope, Gregory IX, placed a personal interdict on Frederick II in an attempt to halt the emperor's growing menace to Rome and to the Church. A few weeks later the soldiers and mercenaries of Frederick II struck swiftly from his stronghold in Lombardy, and Monte Cassino, known to be loyal to the pope, became an armed camp. The abbot and senior monks fled, Thomas with them, his studies brought to an abrupt halt. From the safety of Naples, the abbot sent word to the Count of Aquino that his son was safe, and Thomas returned to the bleak castle of Rocca Sicca which housed the Aquino clan. Italy and the Aquino household were in an uproar and would remain so until after the death of Gregory a year and a half later.

The pillaging of the ancient abbey which drove Thomas Aquinas from his quiet life was but one strategem in a continuing battle between pope and emperor, a battle that began late in the reign of Pope Innocent III when Frederick was elected to the throne of Frederick Barbarossa by the German princes and began a long and intensive campaign to make himself master of Europe.

After Innocent's death, the battle continued with Honorius III and was brought to a fierce pitch in the reign of Gregory who had made a temporary peace with Frederick by the Treaty of San Germano in 1230, the year Thomas entered Monte Cassino. But during the quiet years, Frederick was in Germany bribing princes and pursuing heretics to shield his real intents, preparing for a final assault upon the papal sovereignty. In 1237, he defeated the papal forces in Lombardy and prepared to descend on Rome. The papal interdict of 1239 unleashed Frederick's fury again and a few weeks later his mercenaries were drawn up outside Monte Cassino. He devastated the abbey, held court in the abbey church and drove the monks from their cloister. The next year, the pope would call a general council to depose the emperor, but Frederick's galleys sailing out of Pisa would capture the bishops enroute to the council and hold them prisoner for three years. This battle between pope and emperor would continue until 1245 when the Council of Lyons under Innocent IV would finally break Frederick's power by deposing him, the emperor dying in 1252, a broken and defeated man.

In the company of the exiled monks, Thomas fled to Naples and then joined his family at Rocca Sicca. He was fourteen years old, a large boy, round of face and of enormous girth, wrapped up in an immense silence which was to be his most marked attribute. A year later, his parents, judging him unprepared or unsuited for castle life sent him to the University of Naples. At fifteen, he was useless as a soldier and at Naples he could be trained for service in the court of Frederick II.

## Naples: The Search for Identity

That Thomas Aquinas should be sent to Naples, to the imperial university, is a strange commentary upon the intentions of his family. Monte Cassino had been a stronghold of the papal party, it embodied the best in the Catholic tradition and Thomas had been exposed to it for ten long years. His enrollment at Naples was an added touch of loyalty to the emperor from the Aquino family and they undoubtedly hoped that he would emerge an astute and loyal vassal of the emperor, schooled in law, philosophy and the arts, ready to be of service to the emperor and his court.

Naples in 1241 was the life and light of the Italian peninsula. There the emperor had set up his "University," an odd collection of schools and professorships where prominence was given to the oriental sciences, especially, medicine, and the Greek discipline of the liberal arts. A school of theology was also attached to the University, but the emperor's preference was for more occult studies and he himself presided at student gatherings and sometimes conducted a class on the art and science of falconry.

The University was set up to challenge the eminence of the papal universities of Paris, Bologna, Padua and Oxford, and no family loyal to the emperor would send its son beyond the mountains to the training camp of the enemy. For his parents, Thomas' study at Naples was part of a career in the service of the Hohenstaufen, and they expected that Thomas would eventually advance the fortunes of the Aquino family in the court of Frederick II.

But for Thomas, Naples was a search, a search for his own identity in a sudden move that brought him into manhood and into the "world." It was a rich, exciting, sensual world that he faced, bewildering in its complexity and intense in its passions and loyalties. The flame of idealism that had been born in the solitude of Monte Cassino searched the intellectual landscape of Naples for meaning and expression. As he became a student at the University of Naples, he became a student also of men, of movements and of currents of thought.

He found kinship there in the lecture halls of Petrus Hibernius, an Irish master of the liberal arts and a favorite of Frederick II. This Irish master was a superb teacher and opened to Thomas the lucid writings of Aristotle. In his own search for identity, Thomas found in Petrus Hibernius the passionate lover of objective truth and a teacher who could ignite in his own students the spark of philosophic thinking. At Naples, too, Thomas found professors who were exiled monks from Monte Cassino, giving lectures in philosophy and gathering around them small bands of devoted students. He found also there a new and startingly different kind of monk, a monk who was philosopher, theologian and apostle, whose motto was *Veritas,* and whose apostolate seemed expressly designed to meet the challenge of the times. The white-robed Friars Preachers were new in Naples and new to Thomas. On the whole landscape of Naples, they alone seemed to embody a rationale that faced the present without eclipsing the past. Thomas' search for identity led to the Dominican Church of St. Dominic and face-to-face with a most unusual personality, Johannus Teutonicus — Dominican, bishop and provincial of the Friars Preachers in Lombardy.

## Naples: The Dominican Vocation

Johannus Teutonicus was provincial of Lombardy for the Dominican Order but had special ties with the University of Naples. He was a German and his presence at Naples from time to time was a diplomatic move on the part of the Dominican master-general, Raymond of Penafort, to safeguard the interests of the Dominicans in the imperial city. His visits to Naples, and his lectures there, were not without significance.

As a young professor at the University of Bologna in 1212, Johannus had known the emperor, Frederick II. The emperor at that time was just a young man of sixteen and so magical was his personality that Johannus followed the young emperor back to Germany, attaching himself to his court. At that time, it seemed that the emperor would be the architect of a new dawning of knowledge in Europe and Johannus looked upon him as a new star on the horizon.

It did not take take long for the young professor to become thoroughly disillusioned with the dynamic young Hohenstaufen, as he began to indulge his taste for Moslem beauties and occult sciences, and he returned to Bologna, watching with interest and hope the remarkable pontificate of Innocent III with his daring new ideas for Christendom. In 1219, he succumbed to the magic of a far different man, the intense Spaniard, Dominic of Calereuga, whose new Order of Preachers was still a fresh and daring innovation. All that he had hoped for from Frederick he found embodied in the mind of Dominic. In 1227, he was made Dominican provincial of Hungary, one of the trouble spots of Europe, and finally bishop there. This last step was quite beyond his ambitions and he asked to be relieved of a difficult and nerve-racking assignment where he was only an arbiter between princes and the sole umpire in a series of political feuds that rocked the country.

Because of his acquaintance with Frederick II who carried out his battles against the pope from his stronghold in Lombardy, Johannus was made provincial of Lombardy, but made frequent visits to Naples. The emperor still had a deep regard for his old professor and follower, and the freedom that the Dominicans possessed at Naples and their position at the university were due in most part to Frederick's respect for the intellect of Johannus Teutonicus and his recognition of the uniquely uncommon quality of the Dominican apostolate.

Thomas attended the lectures of the Dominicans. What impressed him about the white-clad friars were their intellects. They were no less men of God than the Benedictines or other monks of the age, but they pursued intellectual excellence with a special passion. Their motto, *Veritas,* sang with an idealism that sank deep into Thomas' soul and he found, as the months went on, that he had a deep and growing kinship with these Dominican preachers and theologians.

His family, apparently, had no knowledge of his growing interest in the mendicant friars, and certainly would not have approved of the interest had they known it. His acquaintance with the apostolic aims and ideals of the Friars Preachers brought him to the threshold of the major decision of his whole life.

### *The War with the Family: Invasion of Privacy*

There were many reasons why the Aquinos would not have approved of his interest in the friars. First of all, these "grubby little beggars," as the Dominicans were called, were intensely loyal to the pope, and any family in the emperor's service would never permit a son or a vassal to ally himself with the enemy camp. The very prospect of such a step would have caused any of Frederick's nobles to blanch with fear, for the wrath of the emperor could be swift and terrible. He had laid waste whole towns and devastated abbeys for much less. Moreover, Thomas had been sent for training to the imperial university to prepare himself for service in the emperor's court, as an astute lawyer perhaps like Piero della Vigna and Thaddeus of Suessa, Frederick's legists, or if a churchman, as an abbot of Monte Cassino. An Aquino trained in the imperial university, an emperor's man, as abbot of the great monastery would carry on in a crucial spot the family's traditional loyalty to Frederick. Both Theodora herself, who ruled the family after her husband's death in 1242, and the emperor were not unmindful of the significance of such a position. Every biographer of Thomas mentions his mother's passionate interest in placing him as abbot of this powerful monastery and her intense rage when she found her wishes frustrated.

When word came to the family at Rocca Sicca of Thomas' reception into the Order of Preachers at the hands of Johannus Teutonicus, Theodora reacted with fearful fury. She took off for Naples at the head of a small army and when she found that Thomas was already on the road to Rome and on his way out of Italy, she gave orders like a general and had her son kidnapped on the road above Rome. Rome itself was in turmoil, for the newly elected pope, Innocent IV, had himself fled Rome, taking refuge in Lyons, in the kingdom of Louis IX, from where he would direct a campaign of politics and strategy which would eventually destroy Frederick.

Johannus Teutonicus, who understood well the nature of the battle that was raging between the emperor and the pope and the significance of Thomas' little part in the drama, was hurrying the son of the Aquinos out of Italy when the mercenaries of Frederick II, led by Thomas' own brothers, Landulf and Raynoldo, swooped down upon them as they rested by the side of the road, not far from the little village of Aquapendente. The young Dominican was forcefully carried to the family's stronghold of San Giovanni, not far from Rocca Sicca, and imprisoned in the old castle until a careful study could be made of the delicate position in which this placed the family. Not only did Theodora see her dreams of family prestige shattered by this rash action of her son, but she feared that the loyalty of the family itself would be questioned if this news reached the ears of Frederick. Apparently, her fears were not without foundation, for Raynoldo, her second youngest son, just a few short years later, for some small indiscretion, was summarily beheaded by Frederick. Theodora had not judged wrongly either her family's dangerous position or the mind of the emperor. She had, however, wrongly judged Thomas, and this massive invasion of his privacy and his chosen destiny brought on a bitter conflict that would eventually be fought in the very presence of the pope.

*The War with the Family: The Open Conflict*

Thomas was but eighteen when he was plunged into the conflict that would decide his whole future destiny, and the tenacity with which he clung to his determined choice angered and exasperated the whole Aquino clan. His habit was ripped from his back by his brothers and his mother, strong-willed and no less determined, used every means to break down his resistance.

For a young man to thus withstand the fury and scheming of the whole family is a testimony to Thomas' spirit and to his singular independence of mind. He was not only kept imprisoned, but brother, sister and mother used every persuasive tactic to bring about a change of mind.

The most subtle of these, it seems, was the scheme of Raynoldo, a student of the love philosophy of the troubadors, and of the romance poets of Provence, with strong overtones from the court of Frederick II. The details of the scheme are not known, but the intent and purpose are revealed in every account of the incident. While the young eighteen-year-old is sleeping, wearied perhaps by long arguments and much loneliness, a young woman his own age is let into his room. Suddenly, unexpected, in the dead of the night, *solus cum sola,* as the moralists repeated in their confessional manuals. Raynoldo must have looked upon himself as a true artist *d'amor,* and he must have relished this exquisite conspiracy with Lady Love. The chastity which Thomas displayed was something quite beyond his comprehension and he certainly must have judged that his brother was somewhat abnormal.

Thomas drove the girl from his room with a burning stick from his fireplace and this example of the barbarism of his family must have thoroughly sickened him, and he began to fight back. He won his sisters to his side, contacted the Dominicans in Naples, obtained books to occupy his mind in solitude, and prepared to wait out the battle.

His mother, meanwhile, had petitioned Innocent IV at Lyons to free her son from the influence of the Dominicans, a strange move considering her family's loyalty to Frederick. This may have brought the family into the bad graces of the emperor who was preparing at this time his mighty defense before the already gathering Council of Lyons. He had prevented such a council three years before by kidnapping a hundred bishops enroute to Rome, but now Louis IX, king of France, made it very clear that if he threatened the pope, the full fury of the French would be unleashed upon him.

Theodora's appeal to the pope may not have pleased him at this critical time. The knowledge that the son of one of his nobles was being kept a prisoner by his own family cannot have been unknown to Frederick's court. The courtiers indeed were ill-prepared to understand the heroism of Thomas' battle for chastity, but his courage and determination must have gained their admiration. His Dominican brethren, too, were not idle. They appealed to the pope for the release of one of their members, and it is not at all impossible that Johannus Teutonicus himself, who had become master-general of the Order in 1241, made a personal appeal to his old pupil, Frederick II, and obtained a favorable hearing. Thomas' release, however, did not come quickly, and he spent over a year in the castle of San Giovanni.

*The War with the Family: The Long Winter*

Thomas Aquinas was caught in the politics of his age. In January, 1245, seven months after his imprisonment in San Giovanni, Innocent IV called a general council to be held at Lyons in June of that year, for the sole purpose of deposing Frederick II. Frederick, in his turn, was busy with his massive mind and corps of legists preparing both a defense of his position and a full scale attack upon the papal position, as he had done previously with the kindly Honorius III. He knew that in Innocent he was dealing with the finest legal mind of the age, and he worked carefully and cautiously in his defense. His aim was to be emperor of the Romans, supreme ruler in Europe and in the confrontation of pope and emperor Lyons would be decisive.

Neither pope nor emperor, it seemed, wished to bring into the arena any factors not directly related to the problem. Theodora's appeal to the pope and Johannus Teutonicus' appeal to Frederick were both diplomatically shelved until the great battle was over. Thomas, meanwhile, with the help of his sisters had obtained another Dominican habit, was in frequent contact with his Dominican brethren at Naples, and may have even received visits from them in secret. In his solitude, he pored over the Bible, obtaining a mastery of its text that would later burst forth in his commentaries and in the *Summa Theologica*. The theological synthesis of Peter Lombard, a primitive attempt compared to Thomas' own later work, he thoroughly digested, and he reveled in the lucid logic of Aristotle whose order and clarity would delight him to the end of his life.

For over a year, until some time after the Council of Lyons in June, 1245, he was kept prisoner by his family; then, after the political defeat of Frederick at Lyons, he was set free. Whether Frederick, whose position was weakened by his condemnation by the council, wished to make concessions to the pope, or whether the family feared to share in the papal wrath now directed against the emperor, is not known. There are indications that his mother sternly opposed his release and it may have been with the connivance of the other members of the family that he was finally released, some say in a basket over the side of the castle. He went immediately to Naples, then to Rome and finally, again in the company of Johannus Teutonicus, over the mountains to Paris.

From this point onwards, there seems to be no further communication by Thomas with his family, at least not until late in life when his two sisters — Marotta, who became a Benedictine nun, and Theodora, who married an Italian nobleman — enter once more into the picture. Even then, it was briefly. The nineteen-year-old boy seems to have severed connections with his family entirely, and with an idealism that would be with him to the very end, became absorbed and wrapped up in the life and labors of the Dominicans.

His struggle, however, and his gifts had been watched and carefully appraised by Johannus Teutonicus who was already writing the charter of the Order's apostolate. He had established language schools and was already training experts in a wide variety of skills and sciences for an expanding apostolic program. During Thomas' imprisonment, the Dominican general chapter had passed critical legislation updating the methods and techniques of their unique Order of Preachers, and they were attracting to their ranks some of the finest minds of the universities. It was in the universities, too, that they had placed their best minds and it was towards the greatest university in the world that Thomas went in the company of the Dominican master-general. He accompanied Johannus to Paris, his mind and his talents ripe for the enriching experience of a great teacher. At Paris was the "great teacher" himself, the *Doctor Universalis,* the most remarkable teacher of the age, Albertus Magnus, the Suabian, who would take the mind of the young Aquino and bring it to brilliant maturity.

## CHAPTER 13

# Stephen Langton: Architect of the Magna Carta

On June 19, 1215, King John of England met in a field at Runnymede with his nobles and courtiers, and at the conclusion of the meeting he had signed the document which is considered the backbone of modern constitutional government and the beginnings of English parliamentary law. On the field at Runnymede that day was the man who was chiefly responsible for the document, one of the greatest churchmen and statesmen in the history of Christianity: Stephen Langton, archbishop of Canterbury.

He was born at Langton, a town near Spilsby in Lincolnshire, about the year 1170, and seems to have inherited the spirit and boldness of St. Thomas a Becket who was martyred that year. His childhood was spent when Henry II ruled England, and he knew the turmoil and confusion of those years. As a young boy, he was sent to Paris to study, since Paris was the center of learning for the whole of Christendom and very early became known for his learning and his holiness.

Langton was remarkable for his knowledge and love of sacred scripture and early in his life was compared to St. Bede the Venerable, who had a like knowledge of the Bible. It is he who is responsible for the division of the Bible into chapters and verses, and his division of the sacred text survives to this day. More than that, however, was he noted for. During the twenty-three years he sat on the see of Canterbury, he produced more commentaries on sacred scripture for his flock than any occupant of the see. He was theologian, canonist, jurist, and left a mark upon English history that endures to this day.

In 1206, the see of Peter was occupied by a man whose apostolic program was to revitalize the Church in a very critical age: Innocent III. Out of his age came the cathedrals of Europe, the beginnings of most of the great European universities, and the spiritual genius of men like St. Francis of Assisi, St. Dominic of Calereuga, St. Louis of France and St. Thomas Aquinas. Searching the whole of Christendom for men to serve the Church in high places, Innocent made Stephen Langton a cardinal, at a very young age, and brought him to Rome to assist the pope in his program of renewal.

The following year, the see of Canterbury became vacant, and English nobility and clergy sent representatives to Rome, to urge the appointment of a candidate that would further their own interests. Pope Innocent, in a surprise move, urged the election of Stephen Langton as archbishop and presided at a chapter meeting of the monks of Canterbury who had come to Rome, seeking a worthy candidate for the office. It would be over six years before Langton would arrive in Canterbury, for the political climate of England was in turmoil, and the king, John, was not happy with his new archbishop.

During his years of waiting, the archbishop was at the Cistercian Abbey of Pontigny, in France, which had housed St. Thomas a Becket himself during a similar conflict with another king of England. From Pontigny, he received news of England, directed the affairs of his see from a distance, and prepared himself spiritually for an ordeal that might have ended like that of his sainted predecessor: in martyrdom. During these years, too, he was becoming thoroughly familiar with the political history and documents of England, and when he arrived in his native country in 1213, he was the most informed jurist of the day, and was determined that the rights of the Church and the rights of English subjects would be recognized in a manner that would never again be called in question.

John was determined that Stephen Langton would never set foot in England, and he was carrying on a battle with Pope Innocent. He was a thoroughly immoral man, and a rapacious king who robbed his subjects at every turn and crushed his own nobles by acts of oppression unparalleled in English history. Pope Innocent, however, was equal to the cunning and treachery of the English monarch, and when his good intentions and decrees for the English people were rejected again and again by King John, Innocent put the whole of England under interdict, a terrible action for a nation, and King John himself was pronounced excommunicate. He was ordered to accept the new archbishop of Canterbury, under pain of losing his kingdom, and when Philip of France began to make plans to carry out the decree of the pope, the king relented, and invited Langton to take possession of his see.

In July, 1213, Stephen Langton landed at Dover, and there the king met him and knelt at his feet for his blessing. On the surface, it seemed that the struggle was over, and there was hope everywhere that King John would begin to rule his people with a sense of justice. But this was not to be, as Langton himself feared, and within a year, the bad will of the king was evident.

Besides his struggle with the Church, the king had been carrying on a bitter battle with his barons, and he refused to recognize concessions that earlier kings had made for the good of his subjects. The barons, recognizing in the new archbishop of Canterbury a strong ally, gathered around him for advice in their struggle, and Langton became the very soul of the movement for liberty. Wrapped up in the struggle were the basic liberty of the Church and the basic liberties of the people. Stephen Langton became the champion of both, and the king began to regret his acceptance of Langton as archbishop.

In August, 1213, Langton had met with a delegation of barons at St. Paul's in London to discuss their grievances against the king, and recommended that they insist upon the recognition of their rights. This action of the archbishop would be misunderstood by Pope Innocent himself, who looked upon King John's earlier submission as a victory for the Church. Langton, more familiar with English history and English common law, became the leader in a movement to secure once and for all English liberties, and the Magna Carta was the result: the first real charter of liberty in European history. At the historic meeting at Runnymede in 1215, King John signed the document, and the first chapter of the constitutional history of England began.

At this point in history, a strange fact occurs. Hearing conflicting reports from England, and not sympathetic with the movement towards confederation in the kingdom of King John, Pope Innocent annulled the Magna Carta, looking upon it as an act of rebellion on the part of John's subjects. He ordered the archbishop of Canterbury to excommunicate the rebellious barons, and this Langton could not do, since he had been their adviser and counselor in that historic confrontation with the king. Preparing to go to Rome to enlighten the pope on the true situation in England, he found himself rebuked and suspended from office. He was on his way to the ecumenical council convoked by the pope when the news reached him, and continued to Rome to present his case to the pope.

He was an able defender of his own actions, and his position was accepted by the pope, but he was advised to remain in Rome until the struggle in England was over. When he finally returned to England in 1218, both Pope Innocent and King John were dead, and a whole new era began for England and for the Church. The rights of the Church and of the English people had been secured, and Langton's last days were spent in labors for his flock fully as important as his struggles with the king.

He worked to consolidate his earlier efforts, and called a provincial synod for which he wrote a body of canons remarkable for their breadth and flexibility. The Church council that he opened at Osney in 1222 is considered as important to the ecclesiastical history of England as the Magna Carta is to its constitutional history. The Lateran Council called by Innocent in 1215 had been a mighty, reforming council and Stephen Langton made its decrees effective in England.

The latter days of Langton saw a blossoming of the faith in England almost unequalled in English history. It was during these years that the first Dominicans and Franciscans, who spearheaded Church renewal in those days, arrived in England. Stephen Langton welcomed both groups, and saw in their spirit and apostolic zeal a vital new instrument for furthering the work of the Church. During these last years, also, the University of Oxford became a vital force in the intellectual life of

Christendom, and would almost rival the University of Paris as a center of learning. During these years, when the young king, Henry III, was preparing for the serious work of ruling England, the principles embodied in the Magna Carta became the common law of England, and Langton saw his work and his convictions blossom into an era of prosperity and peace.

Three phases in the life of Stephen Langton divide the labors of this great man. His early years were spent in study and teaching, where he acquired a luminous knowledge of the scriptures that would be the nourishment and strength of his later labors. In 1206, he begins his life as statesman and jurist, and through a long and painful struggle succeeds in delivering England from the rule of tyrants and giving it a remarkable juridic document, the most amazing political document in European history. And finally, the last ten years of his life, filled with pastoral labors, revitalizing the religious life of the English people, and laying the foundation for some of its greatest religious institutions.

When he died in 1228, he had been archbishop of Canterbury for twenty-two years, and England and the Church were about to enter upon what many consider the greatest age in the history of the Church: "the Thirteenth, Greatest of Centuries." This age was remarkable for its saints, for its theologians, its statesmen, its religious genius, its flowering of the arts and its advances in political history. At Oxford, Roger Bacon would lay the foundations for empiric science and at Paris, where Stephen Langton had studied and taught, St. Albert the Great and St. Thomas Aquinas would open a new era for theology. The spiritual fire of St. Francis of Assisi would inflame the whole of Europe and the Catholic Norsemen would plant the faith on the distant shores of Greenland.

His contemporaries found it difficult to describe the stature and the genius of Langton. He embodied in himself so many diverse elements and accomplished so well such a great variety of tasks, that he had no parallel in their immediate memory. In his learning, they compared him to Bede; in his statesmanship, to Justinian; and in his labors for his flock, to other great English bishops: St. Wulfstan, St. Thomas a Becket and St. Hugh of Lincoln. He combined in himself the English love of liberty and the Roman love of order, and his Magna Carta is an unusual blend of firmness and flexibility in facing the tasks of the body politic.

There are those who have claimed that the Church and churchmen have had no love for individual liberties, and that Church authorities have always sided with governments in their oppression of peoples. The history of Stephen Langton, following so closely upon that of St. Thomas a Becket, is shining proof to the contrary. In his own lifetime, inspired by his own familiarity with the mind of God as reflected in sacred scripture, he fought for the liberty of his people, and in the Magna Carta he passed on a heritage of *law* and *justice* which has been the very lifeblood of constitutional law. The architect of the Magna Carta, modeling his life and labors upon that of the Good Shepherd, thus becomes the lawgiver of the ages, extending the reign of Christ down through the centuries, and showing that divine wisdom is always the finest and best safeguard for the workings of human wisdom.

## CHAPTER 14

# Portrait of a Contemplative

St. Stephen Harding has been called an intellectual, a scholar, a puritan, a stoic — none of which describe him fairly or accurately. He was called none of these in his own lifetime. That he was scholarly, there is no doubt, for he has left ample evidence of this. That he was an intellectual is also evident, though not in the sense some attach to the word. He was educated, well-educated; courteous, kindly, gentle in manner; characteristics inherited from his Anglo-Saxon monastic heritage. He had none of the mercurial extremes in his temperament for which his disciple, Bernard of Clairvaux, was noted, but he was fully as brilliant, endowed with qualities of leadership the Cistercian Order did not see again for another century, and was a man of pointed and fiery convictions.

He was appreciated more in the generation that followed him than he would ever be again in Cistercian history. This generation described him as *Dux et Signifer Ordinis,* the "Prince and Standard-bearer of the Order." The title is not without significance.

It is a strange commentary on Cistercian history that his rare and monumental achievement has been questioned or ignored by those who profited most by his labors. It is as if the Dominicans were to forget St. Dominic, or the Franciscans, St. Francis. It is an even stranger commentary on Cistercian history that St. Bernard of Clairvaux has replaced Stephen Harding in Cistercian devotion and hagiography. Historically, this is probably explained by the fact that the Abbey of Clairvaux very early challenged the position of the Mother-Abbey of Citeaux as mother and head of the Cistercian Order. This conflict did not grow into a schism, but it did obscure the face and figure of one of the greatest monastic geniuses in the history of Christianity.

Stephen Harding was English, Saxon, from Dorsetshire in south England. He was quiet, studious, gentle and affable. He was by nature fitted for a contemplative life, and his whole life was an impassioned search for a genuine contemplative existence. Exactly what contemplative life is, is today the subject of warm and wide debate, but it is not difficult to understand what Stephen Harding sought in such a life. He sought for a life in which the presence of God was fostered with genius; in which the whole of life was rooted in a vibrant and living knowledge of God, at once personal and objective; a life in which (in today's terminology) theology was the dominant occupation of the monk, a theology which blossomed into an intense life of prayer and kept the monk in an habitual companionship with God.

This quality of St. Stephen Harding's mind, which was the root and principle of Cistercian monasticism, has found its best expression, to my knowledge, in a penetrating study of St. Thomas Aquinas which appeared in *La Vie Spirituelle* several years ago. The writer, Thomas Deman, O.P. says this of his brother Dominican:

> "In the case of the majority of saints, sanctity and knowledge seem to be two different things ... and as a general rule, we do not realize that intellectual excellence may have a connection with the merits which raise a Christian to the altars. The interest of the case of St. Thomas Aquinas is that we are compelled to investigate the problem. ... Among all possible objects, St. Thomas chose to know God. We can bring back to that one point the accumulation of knowledge that he carried in his mind. ... Among all objects of knowledge, God is the one possessing singular excellence. For the mind, He is the most wonderful and inexhaustible of objects. He fills man with astonishment and wonder. He forces him to conceive of a beauty and perfection far beyond ... this world. In the sphere of the intellect St. Thomas became a kind of companion of God. He kept to his solitude to live ... in such company."

*To live habitually in the company of God:*

nothing describes better the contemplative ideal of St. Stephen Harding.

Stephen Harding belonged supremely to the Thomistic race of contemplatives, and it is noteworthy that scattered all through the writings of St. Thomas is an exposition and defense of this kind of monastic existence. St. Thomas, in fact, knows no other kind of contemplative life, and the Cistercian Order was created to foster this profound and personal kind of contemplative life.

What one writer has written about the intellect of John Kennedy could be written just as accurately of Stephen Harding: "He was objective, practical, ironic, skeptical, unfettered and insatiable." He was also bold, original, daring, unconventional and untiring. His pragmatic sense was rooted in a profound theological vision, and this wedding of pragmatics and theology, rare in our age but just as rare in his own, was the energizing force of his genius, and is stamped on everything he wrote and in the style and design of his contemplative creation.

There is no place that he reveals himself more than in a touching and spiritually frank letter which he wrote to the abbot of Sherborne shortly before he died. Sherborne had been his home and it was there that he discovered God and was nourished by a rich contemplative life. He left Sherborne to find or to build a dream, and when the dream was accomplished, he wrote back to those who had guided him in his first steps towards God. The Latin of the letter is lucid and quivers with feeling. These are his words:

"Writing letters makes those who are absent seem present and joins in affection those separated by long distances. In the deepest part of my being, I feel that I have never left you, for you took me in as a little child at Sherborne, and educated me carefully and tenderly. When I came across the ocean, you had stamped me with the image of yourself, and I carried with me as a God-given treasure all that you had shown and taught me, spurring me on to accomplish great things. Whatever I am and have, has come from you, and now I ask that you who nourished me in the ways of God will ask God boldly for even greater things. For I have not labored in vain and the harvest of forty long years spreads out before my eyes, as I look forward to death and the reward of working in the Lord's vineyard.

"And so do not let the good things you have heard about us lessen the fervor of your prayers for us. For our labors are not over, and we wish to go forward, chastely and humbly, not lessening our fervor, clinging with all our thought and feeling to God, until he satisfies us with the vision of Himself, which is the goal of all our labors."

No commentary could be a more eloquent witness to his strong and vibrant spirit than these words written at the end of a long life.

For most of his life, Stephen Harding worked against the grain of the obvious. He was at odds with his times, with his contemporaries, and with popular notions. He created a climate for change, and stepped progressively from a minor figure in the drama to a leading force. His strength was in his vision, which knew precisely what it wanted, which could carefully distinguish between the essentials of monastic life and the supplements of men's devising, and could boldly depart from the conventional when the conventional stood in the way.

His arsenal of ideas was scattered through some of the most amazing documents in the history of monasticism, ideas which in his own time were highly revolutionary and were drawn from no existing tradition. He appears on the scene, does his unique work, and departs. When he came upon the scene, there was chaos, anarchy and spiritual stagnation. When he leaves the scene, there is order, unity and a rich spiritual awakening, setting the world aflame with sanctity. In the generation that followed him were born Becket, St. Hugh of Lincoln, Stephen Langton and St. Dominic. All felt the influence of his spiritual genius and each, in some way, resembles him. It is significant that two of them, Thomas a Becket and Stephen Langton, both sought refuge and solitude in the monastery founded by Stephen Harding's favorite disciple, Hugh of Macon, at Pontigny. And it would not be historically inaccurate to see more than a verbal resemblance between the Carta Caritatis of Stephen Harding and the Magna Carta of Stephen Langton.

By nature, he grasped the larger view and he maneuvered the Cistercian reform, which in its externals resembled many other reforms taking place at the same time, into its historical position with all the insight and adroitness of a power politician. His grasp upon human affairs, apparently, was phenomenal, and this is not surprising considering that his contemporaries were men of the stature of Hildebrande (Gregory VII), Lanfranc and Anselm of Canterbury, Bruno of Cologne, the notorious Ranulph of Bessin (Flambard), and the key figure of his age, William the Conqueror. It is also not surprising considering his intellectual and monastic genealogy. Contributing to the spiritual personality of Stephen Harding were the luminous and lovable Cuthbert of Lindisfarne, Benedict Biscop, Bede the Venerable, Dunstan of Canterbury and Alfred the Great. One generation removed from him saw a figure who resembled him more closely than any of these: St. Wulfstan, the Saxon bishop who survived the Norman conquest, with his courage, his personality, his boldness and his wit intact. There was a biting edge to Stephen Harding's personality, but it was softened by his Saxon breeding and especially by his contemplative vision.

If he accomplished nothing else for medieval monasticism, he created options. His option, he felt, was as valid as that presented by Cluny. In doing so, he challenged Cluny's monopoly in monastic matters and brought down upon his followers the intense hatred of the abbots of Cluny, until St. Bernard of Clairvaux and Peter the Venerable made peace. Even then, it was Stephen Harding's option that made the most sense. Other options followed upon his and from his boldness came variety. His monastic declaration of independence inspired other revolutions from the Cluniac empire.

What set him apart in the twelfth century was a tenacity of purpose in seeking his own rendezvous with destiny; he saw no reason why evil and greedy men should have a monopoly on boldness, and noted that worldly-minded and ambitious men found little to oppose their schemes, and that their schemes usually succeeded. Right before his eyes he had the example of Flambard, the henchman of William Rufus, whose boldness in pure malevolence rocked the age. Stephen rocked it, too, and his boldness matched and surpassed that of Flambard.

Stephen Harding was the total contemplative. Intensely passionate, he rooted his energies in God and opened his whole being to His splendor. This passion for God shot a wind of fury through his bones and brought him face-to-face with the breathtaking reality of eternal life. Faith to him was knowledge, knowledge made vibrant by an insatiable curiosity that constantly plumbed the depths of theological knowledge and carved monuments of wonder in his mind. From this came a style of life noticed by all around him, remarked on even by men a century removed from him. The truth which he grasped and lived by, he emblazoned on his age in the Order of Citeaux, and scrawled across the face of his century a message that impressed itself into the very stones of his monasteries.

This unmistakable mystique, profoundly

theological, but intensely personal, molded the Cistercian Order into a unique entity. Cistercian life was totally contemplative and this set it apart from the other monastic institutions of the age.

The young prophet who shook the dust of Molesme from his sandals and challenged the monastic empire of Cluny, mellowed and matured into the old visionary whose eyes searched the horizons for the promised land and waited for the coming of the Lord in thunder. His eyes always seemed to be shy with secrets and the intensity of his expectations was evident even on his deathbed, when he looked back only once: to wonder if he had shared his vision as mightily as he might. After he died, Burgundy burned with his memory and legends were created, larger than life, but not larger than the memory.

The sanctity of St. Stephen Harding was a rare contemplative sanctity, shot through with a theological directness reflected in Thomas a Becket and Thomas Aquinas: eminently human, sane, adventurous, impassioned and original. He had prepared himself for his role in history, not directly by foreseeing his future labors, but by pursuing sharply defined goals and committing himself to a definite intellectual and contemplative tradition. This commitment he never forsook and this tenacity is characteristic of his sanctity.

At a time when Western Christendom was disillusioned and in near despair, he appeared, recovered lost hopes and quickened aspirations into reality. In his lifetime, Godfrey de Bouillon stormed Jerusalem and called half the youth of

Europe to his banner. Stephen stormed the new Jerusalem and his white Cistercian habit became a vibrant and scintillating symbol of a challenge greater than Godfrey's.

## CHAPTER 15

# The Gentle St. Bede

Less than a century after the arrival of St. Augustine in England, there flourished in that part of England called Northumbria, a remarkable Christian civilization, the ruins of which can still be seen here and there in the countryside. Much of it was the work of a remarkable English abbot, Benedict Biscop, who brought from Rome and from the continent the best ecclesiastical traditions and built here in the heart of England a Catholic culture that would nourish the English nation for almost a thousand years.

Great names would dot the heritage: Alfred the Great; Alcuin, the schoolmaster of Charlemagne; Stephen Langton, the architect of the Magna Carta; St. Thomas a Becket; Oxford University; St. Thomas More. But the name that heads the list, and one of the most beautiful products of this amazing era was a gentle, learned, kindly man who never left his monastery and who wrote, in that far distant age, books of history, theology and scriptural commentary that passed on to later generations the richness and wisdom of the faith.

His name was Baeda, but it has come down to us as Bede, and for centuries, he was known simply as Bede the Venerable. The great Benedict Biscop had built two monasteries, one at Wearmouth and one at Jarrow, not far apart; Wearmouth was inland and Jarrow relatively close to the sea. Bede entered the monastery as a very young boy, and spent most of his life at Jarrow, praying and studying and sharing his knowledge with his fellow monks. In his greatest work, the *Ecclesiastical History of the English People,* he describes himself and his labors:

> "I, Baeda, a servant of God and priest of the monastery of the blessed Apostles Peter and Paul, which is at Wearmouth and Jarrow, being born in the territory of the same monastery, was given by kinsfolk at seven years of age to be educated by the most reverend Abbot Benedict ... spending the remainder of my life in that monastery, I wholly applied myself to the study of the scriptures. Amid the observances of the rule and the daily charge of singing in the Church, I ever took delight in learning and teaching and writing."

Little is known of his parentage, but, as was the custom in those days, he was offered to the monastery by his parents, using the touching ceremony described in the *Rule of St. Benedict*. When he was very young, perhaps not more than twelve years old, an epidemic struck the monastery and the old abbot and the young boy buried one by one the monks who died, and then took their places dutifully in choir to pray the divine office.

His education, like that of St. Thomas Aquinas, centuries later, was wholly monastic. The daily drama of the liturgy, the constant reading of the scriptures, the familiarity with the writings of the fathers of the Church, and his own pondering of the sacred text gave him a luminous wisdom and gracious style that lives even today and had a wide influence even in his own lifetime. Alcuin, when helping Charlemagne to build schools in his kingdom, treasured his writings and several councils of bishops during the Middle Ages placed a high value on his theological labors.

He was probably the most learned man of his time, and his historical writings make him the Father of English History. He was very careful in research and consulted every authority available before putting his facts on paper. His greatest joy, it seems, was his exposition of sacred scripture and his homilies and commentaries reflect his calm, contemplative spirit and his love of the sacred text.

Throughout his writings, he often bursts into prayer, and these have been preserved in his manuscripts. In one place, he writes: "And I pray You, loving Jesus, that as You have graciously given me to drink in with delight the words of Your knowledge, so You would kindly grant me to attain one day to You, the foundation of all wisdom and appear forever before Your face." This longing for eternity, which is characteristic of the contemplative mind, is evident throughout his writings, and in this he resembles St. Thomas Aquinas, who towards the end of his life had to lay down his pen, so great was his yearning for God. This longing is reflected in this prayer of St. Bede, yet sobered by his Anglo-Saxon reserve: "Grant, O Christ, I beseech You, of Your grace, that Your good spirit may lead me in the right way . . . that . . . I may search into the commandments of my God, and with the eyes of my mind awakened, may go forward faithfully to read and to weigh the marvels of Your holy law."

His interests, however, were not narrowly monastic. His historical writings and biographies are filled with interesting and accurate observations of the world around him, and he even wrote treatises on musical theory and harmony. He wrote poetry, short treatises on science, as it was known in his time, and short studies on the art of history. His greatest work, and the one that has enshrined him in the halls of the great, is his *Ecclesiastical History of the English People* and this alone is a remarkable piece of writing for its time. In it, he gives an account of Christianity in England from the beginnings until his own day, and this work is the foundation of all our knowledge of early English history and a masterpiece eulogized by scholars of every age.

At the age of nineteen, he was ordained deacon, and at thirty, he was raised to the priesthood, becoming what was known in those days as a "Mass priest." Not every monk was a priest; but an abbot would usually select for ordination only enough priests to care for the spiritual needs of the community. Bede was one of these, and he seems to have been a teacher of the younger monks and his main occupation was the study of scripture and the exposition of the sacred text for the members of his community. In order to do this more fruitfully, however, he studied and wrote of anything that would clarify or illuminate the scriptures themselves, and he passed his knowledge onto his contemporaries.

Nestled in the hills of Northumbria, this monastic civilization, however, was not destined to endure. Not long after Bede's death, the Vikings would sweep down through England, destroying everything. They would ravage Lindisfarne, to the north, another sacred place, where St. Cuthbert had died, and Cuthbert's followers would take his body and carry it from place to place for over 200 years until they found a safe place to enshrine it. Wearmouth and Jarrow, too, would be destroyed and England would enter a dark age and for a time, Bede's memory would be forgotten. Later, King Alfred the Great, trying to rebuild the faith in England, would recover his memory.

St. Bede died at about the age of sixty-five and the account of his death is touching. On the eve of the Ascension, sensing that he did not have much time to live, he gathered his disciples around him. He held a box of treasures that he had saved for this moment and he wanted to give them to those who were remaining behind: spice and incense and embroidered linen. He had labored, he told them, because "I would not that my children should learn a lie" and he would labor even to his dying breath. He had been dictating a translation of St. John's Gospel to one of his young disciples, Wilbert, and as he paused in his dictation, the young boy said: "There is still one sentence, dear master, which is not written down." When Bede had dictated the last sentence, the boy said: "Now it is finished."

"You have spoken the truth," Bede answered. "It is finished. Take my head in your hands for it much delights me to sit opposite any holy place where I used to pray, and so sitting to call upon my Father." The young boy helped him to rise and Bede knelt upon the floor of his cell singing the *Gloria Patri*. When he had finished, he died in the arms of his disciple.

Very soon after his death, he was called Venerable and it is only in modern times that he has received the final crown of his labors. In 1859, Cardinal Wiseman of England, petitioned the Holy See that St. Bede be declared a Doctor of the Church. Thirty years later, in the pontificate of Pope Leo XIII, who had a special place in his heart for the English, St. Bede's name was added to the Church's list of Doctors, those especially noted for their holy lives and their holy teaching. In England, and in monastic communities, he had been so honored for centuries, and but for the devastations of the Vikings shortly after his death, he would undoubtedly have been so honored soon after his death.

His writings, after the dark Viking years were over, spread quickly through the whole of Europe and many of his homilies were incorporated into the readings of the divine office. Priests and monks were guided by his writings for centuries and his Latin is simple and lucid and very easy to follow. He left his warm and gentle personality on every page of his writings, and he is a shining example of that sane and gentle English sanctity which would later be reflected in men like Stephen Langton, St. Thomas More, and in modern times, in G. K. Chesterton.

Today, the monastery where he lived is just a ruin on a hillside. In 794, the Norsemen came ashore all over England, and burned the house where Bede had lived and ransacked it. Since that day, it has lain silent in the meadows of Northumbria, its stones scattered over the hillside.

The body of Bede, however, for centuries has been preserved in another place. When the Danes invaded Lindisfarne, the home of St. Cuthbert, in 773, the little colony of monks who lived there took flight. With them they carried the body of the saint who had been monk and bishop and then solitary. Their journey continued for over two centuries, the monks hiding in caverns and guarding the body of their monastic father. Since Cuthbert had been bishop, wherever the body rested, the see of Cuthbert would be set up, and the monks' superior became the bishop of the region. In 990, the monks and the body of Cuthbert finally came to rest at Durham, in north England, not far from the Scottish border. First, a small stone monastery was built to house the holy remains, but in 1109 was begun the great cathedral of Durham, one of the great masterpieces of medieval architecture.

Today, St. Bede's body rests with that of Cuthbert in the crypt of Durham cathedral. For centuries, of course, it was a Catholic cathedral, but after the Reformation in England at the time of Henry VIII, the cathedral was placed in the hands of the Anglican Church, which has custody of the shrine today.

What is significant today is that St. Bede was the product of that contemplative life which enriched the Church for centuries. He never left his monastery; his chief concern was the round of monastic duties and the studies that formed and nourished his own spiritual life. The monk was a man intent upon God and eternal life, and he pursued God with the full bent of his intelligence, the full vigor of his will, and with all the intensity and passion of his soul. The monastic life, in Bede's day, was primarily a life of deep companionship with God, a companionship that led ultimately to the very vision of God in eternal life.

It was this vision, seen but dimly by faith, that Bede shared with his contemporaries, and it is this vision that is glimpsed in his life and writings 1,200 years after his death.

## CHAPTER 16

# Joseph the Magnificent

The St. Joseph that most of us know is a composite of late medieval piety and early French spirituality, and so it is difficult in this time of changing religious fashions to write of him with force and conviction. Little is known of his true history and in the heat and battle of making him the model of just about everything in the Catholic Church, it is forgotten that the Joseph who moves through the first pages of the Gospel was a very young man, almost a teen-ager.

He was perhaps eighteen or twenty, Jewish in every respect, a man who lived from a very young age perpetually on the threshold of mystery. Most men at this age live on the threshold of marriage and its widening wonder, but St. Joseph was caught up in a drama more awe-inspiring than the drama of bride and groom and more absorbing than the preoccupations of young love.

He was also caught up in a political turmoil that eventually split his nation right down the middle and for a young man, he was called upon to make some rather pressing and painful decisions. What it was that matured him and what the elements were that went into his education, we do not know. But at a very young age he displayed rare qualities of leadership and the ability to make judgments and decisions for which there had been no precedent in his own life.

His nation, at the time of the birth of Jesus, was the political football of the family of Herod, who ruled Palestine with a mandate from the Roman emperor. Not many years later, the mandate would be withdrawn and the Romans would divide the power of the family, giving Galilee to another Herod, an adjoining territory to his brother, Philip, and taking over the governorship of Judea themselves. St. Luke in his Gospel is careful to indicate these historical and geographical facts. St. Joseph had to live with them.

With the birth of Jesus, Joseph moved into the shadow of death himself, for the half-crazy Herod, disturbed by a prophecy that he would lose his throne, saw everyone as a threat, even his own sons. Herod at this time ruled the whole of Palestine and so a return to Galilee and Nazareth, the home of Mary and Joseph, after the birth of Christ, would not have put them out of danger. Joseph fled the country, taking his wife and her Child with her. When the danger was past, upon the death of the older Herod, Joseph returned.

It is wrong to think that Joseph was so absorbed in the divine drama in which he played so great a part that he was oblivious to the human drama around him. Like other Hebrew people, he was conscious of the divine hand upon the destiny of his race; he knew the promises and the magnificent hope of Israel, and the painful turmoil in the nation must have deeply distressed him. Like all devout Jews, he must have wondered why God had been silent in Israel for more than 500 years; there had been no prophet in all that time to speak of God's interest to His chosen people. Not only that, but their country had been invaded by a foreigner, the Romans, and their rulers were not even Hebrews.

He knew of the promised Messiah and he must have wondered how God would step into history to deliver His people and to restore the kingdom of David to its ancient glory. Like all patriotic Jews, he wanted freedom for his people, but during his whole lifetime there was no sign that such freedom would come.

Joseph's part in the divine drama of the Incarnation, then, must be seen in the light of the history of Israel itself, and his own hopes for his people were not unlike the hopes of any other Jew. His part in the drama is obscure and he moves almost like a shadow through the pages of scripture. But his young mind steeped in the history of Israel must have been fired with a rich new hope when he was initiated, as the Gospels indicate, into the plan of God, and his closeness to the mystery of the Redemption and to the divine event of the Incarnation must have had a profound influence upon his character and personality. Besides this, he must have been a remarkable young man to have been chosen for the role that he was to play.

Later on, in the public life of Jesus Himself, it is quite evident that Jesus' concept of the identity of Israel and the concept shared by the Pharisees and the other official teachers of Israel are quite different. By a teaching campaign unparalleled in the history of Israel, Jesus recovers the magnificent hope of Israel and stirs in God's people a new understanding of their dignity and their destiny. Surely we can see in this part of the personality of Christ a strong echo of that Israelite who must have exemplified in himself the finest characteristics of the true Israelite. Joseph, in his own way and in his own time, must have been the light of the world and the salt of the earth and he must have lived, as few Israelites before him, the dream and the promise that God had given to Israel.

Jesus showed Israel to be, not just the holder of an ancient promise and the privileged one among the nations of the world, but particularly and peculiarly the *Bar Jahve,* the "son of the great God," the begotten of God in human history, destined to bring to the whole of humanity a vision of its dignity and its destiny, embodying in itself, not just the legal prescriptions of the Torah, but all those characteristics of the beloved of God and all those endowments that make for a rich humanity. That this concept clashed with the legalism of the Scribe and the separatism of the Pharisee is the most evident fact of the Gospels themselves. That Joseph must have embodied in himself Jesus' own vision of the true Israelite is an insight that makes the study of St. Joseph an unusual and exciting personality study.

The humanity of St. Joseph, at once tender and strong, shaped in the crucible of doubt and decision, nourished on the superb pedagogy of the Psalms of David, riveted in a strong consciousness of God by his whole Hebrew heritage, and buttressed by a sense of the divine presence itself in his life, must have been a fitting companion to the humanity of Jesus Himself. The interchange of companionship and conversation, over long years and in the midst of sharp political and social upheaval, yet on the threshold of a deep and startling divine mystery, must have brought about an enriching familiarity unique in the history of friendships. The Gospels, of course, are silent on these matters, but the bond between Jesus and His foster-father must have been deep and strong.

To us today, certainly, it is the young Joseph, scarcely on the threshold of manhood, wide-eyed in wonder at the mystery accomplished in his young wife, uncertain of the future, yet quivering with an expectancy of the divine, that is especially appealing. His love for the woman of his choice brought with it a challenge unprecedented in the history of man and drew him into a maze of human and divine intrigue that would shape the course of history. The scriptures show him as almost a silent witness to the drama of Redemption, but his part in it called for decisive action, rare human skills and a brilliant appraisal of very difficult situations. The characteristics which he displayed give him kinship, not so much to the silent, meditative saints of popular hagiography, but rather with those vibrant youth of the '60s who flocked to the Peace Corps with a variety of skills to meet a new challenge.

As we learn more of the human dimensions of the Gospels and as our knowledge of the exact geographical and historical background broadens and deepens, so, too, does our knowledge of those persons who are bound up in the drama of Redemption. We must see them as real people, facing true human situations, grappling with problems as real and as pressing as our own. They are not spared the labor of body and intellect that ordinary human life requires and the judgments and decisions they make shape their character and personality as surely as our judgments and decisions shape ours.

St. Joseph has to be seen in the human context in which he lived, grappling with his history and his times, moving across the landscape of a definite time and era. When the history of his time is studied carefully and his part in the drama of the Redemption begins to unfold, then his figure begins to emerge from the fog of history and he is seen to be an amazing man, young in age, alert to currents of history that escape us, decisively shaping the human existence of even the Son of God Himself.

The Joseph that emerges is a fitting model for the Church of today, faced with new and unparalleled challenges, called upon to make decisions unprecedented in her history. It is not without a certain divine rationale that he is the patron of the universal Church, and it is to be hoped and expected that as the Church in this age gains a new knowledge of herself and her mission to mankind, she will bring to her task an energy and a spirit not unlike that of her patron. On the spur of the moment, he followed the divine call into the darkness, ready to face whatever challenges that history would thrust upon him. The Church can do no less, and the challenges that she has to face can be no less decisive for humanity than those that faced the remarkable young man who became the foster-father of Jesus.

## CHAPTER 17

# Portrait of the God-Bearer

The Mother of Jesus had always known the tension of opposites: virginity and motherhood, joy and suffering, the black agony of crucifixion and the white glory of Resurrection. Her womb would always hold the scar of her motherhood, just as His flesh would always hold the scar of His bond with her. Her bond to Him was not just spiritual, it was biological and historical.

This bond with the divine she would bring with her into the exile that brought her to Ephesus, caught up in the drama of a new age, watching the birth of a new Israel. For thirty years, hers had been a life of ordered tranquillity, hers a dark secret to be shared with no one. Virgin, yet mother to a Son whose origin was wrought in a mystery scarcely known even to her. "My spirit leaps with joy in God, my Savior," she had sung. Hovering over her and Him was a darker secret than the one she held.

This bond with the divine was the unique source of her strength, and the memory of those years shed light upon the long years of exile. His physical presence had been taken away and she lived in the shadow of that presence as a vast new age began to dawn.

Mary, the God-bearer, stands with ponderous loneliness as the Spirit of God begins to hover over redeemed humanity and she embodies in her person the meaning and the startling significance of His coming. The flowering of her hope and expectation are lost in the huge silence of her years at Ephesus, but great minds like Ephraim of Syria and great poets like Chesterton have caught a faint glimpse of that massive passion that made her the mistress of the Seraphim.

For her, prayer was an agony of expectation, and faith a prolonged silence, deepening with the years, heavy with a wonder and a tenderness that sharpened into ecstasy when certain memories stirred her. Her intellect was burdened with no idle fancies or suppressed fears, but with a clarity that was a remnant of man's lost golden age; she looked forward to the brilliant fulfillment of the promise of His Resurrection.

No man or woman in history had a part in mankind's destiny as meaningful or as massive as her own, and the afterglow of those naked realities of which she was a part must have riveted in her consciousness a rare and vibrant sense, giving her identity with something larger than the universe.

Her point of entry into history was the historic Incarnation and it is in the white light of history that we must try to grasp the significance of her person. In her, theological dimension and historical dimension are one: *Theotokos* is at once the description of her role in history and the theological definition of her place in the economy of Redemption. She is bound up, in a way that is huge and indescribable, in the Incarnation and Resurrection of the Son of God, and as the new wine of Pentecost begins to shoot through the veins of humanity, she is the one lone observer of the mystery of His Person and His origins.

The connection between her role as God-bearer and her mission to humanity lies deep in the consciousness of Catholics. She was the co-laborer of the Holy Spirit in God's greatest human task: the flesh-taking of God Himself; and she is bound up essentially in the very rationale of Redemption. Moreover, in her God-bearing, she was not just a passive instrument. Her whole being bent to His intentions, every human faculty and every divine gift was absorbed in this mighty task, and she thus becomes the model of all who seek God, for she was a conscious, living instrument of God's will.

Her theological profile is as vast as theology itself since she is at the very heart of the one central event of theology. Her mind and her person, indeed, are a prism of theology and there is reflected in both her mind and her person the impact and the dimensions of the Incarnation itself.

She was not only initiated, as were the apostles and prophets, into God's unspeakable counsel, but she wove for Him from her own physical being the physical fibers of His human nature and stood in the presence of that divine mind as it unfolded the deepest drama of human destiny. The hidden ties binding humanity to God are inextricably woven into the very fabric of her existence, and that special divine genius which we call the Holy Spirit wove round her the vast design of God's new covenant with man.

In the carrying out of His divine plan for the human race, God has peopled history with rare personalities, magnificent mirrors of His own mind and person. Moses, David, the prophets, Paul — all capture something rich and meaningful, reflecting the vastness and the magnitude of the divine intention. It is no small wonder that artists, sculptors, poets of every century have tried with the elements of their art to capture something of the significance of Mary, since she is in a sense a synthesis of the old and new covenants. In her, first and most uniquely, are God's ancient promises fulfilled and new promises made. She captures in her person and in her God-bearing, the full significance of priest, prophet and apostle and is a shining monument to the action of God upon human history. In her role and title of God-bearer, *Theotokos,* is to be found the key to her historical and theological riches, for it is the sole source of her glory and the sole reason why "all generations shall call her blessed."